THE
GRACE
AGENT

God's Mission To
And Through An
Unlikely Vessel

Rick S. Bell

The Grace Agent:

God's Mission To and Through An Unlikely Vessel

ISBN-13: 978-1544100036
ISBN-10: 1544100035

Copyright © 2017 by Rick S. Bell

*This book is dedicated
to all who have faithfully prayed and supported us
through the years. This is partly your story as well as
ours. Any good that God has done through us is also
credited to your account.*

ACKNOWLEDGMENTS

Special thanks to my wife Jennifer for her editorial input in this book, as well as her patient participation with me in life. I love you, my southern Bell!

Thanks to Peter Snyder for encouraging me to write my story.

And "thanks be to God, who gives us the victory through our Lord Jesus Christ" (1Corinthians 15:57).

Contents

Chapter 1

Sometimes It Takes A While

It was a cool, starry night on a college campus in China. Several students gathered outside to practice their spoken English, and we started to talk about the Lord. Finally, a spiritual conversation! Up until that point, they had shown little interest in discussing important topics.

It was going well until a girl, whose English name was Melody, came along and began to argue with me. Melody was absolutely sure that God didn't exist, and she rattled off her objections. As I tried my best to answer her, the rest of the group lost interest and left. She had ruined everything! After that, it seemed I was getting nowhere with her, and we were just wasting time.

Then it happened. All of a sudden, her entire face changed. She began to glow, and she completely changed her tune!

"Now I understand! Now I understand!" she exclaimed, "God DOES exist, and you came here to tell us about Him!"

It was as if heaven had interrupted the conversation and instantly opened her eyes. It had nothing to do with what I was saying. Something clearly supernatural took place.

Nonetheless, Melody wasn't ready yet to put her faith in Jesus, but I still gave her a Bible and encouraged her to read the gospels. She eagerly complied.

A few days later, I ran into her. "Hi, Melody! How's it going with the Bible?"

"Oh, I'm sorry, Mr. Rick," her face turned sad. "I was reading it in the library, and a man asked me what I was doing. I told him, 'I'm reading the Holy Bible and learning about God.' He then got angry and pointed his finger at me, saying, 'You must not do that! That is not for Chinese people.'"

"That's wrong!" I replied. "Don't let that guy steal eternal life from you. Jesus gave Himself for the world and loves ALL people. Keep seeking the truth!"

My pep talk didn't help. She was busy and about to graduate, so she didn't bring up the matter again. The semester ended, I went back to America for a furlough, and Melody moved on.

The year was 2001. Email and cell phones weren't as accessible for students back then, so there was no easy way to keep in touch. Still, I ran into several former students over the years and had some great reunions. But I couldn't find Melody. I would ask others about her, but to no avail. Time went on and it seemed we'd never reconnect. Even so, she'd sometimes come to mind and a prayer would go up for her.

Fast forward to 2016.

I texted a friend from a remote part of China. "This place I'm at is dark and creepy. I just want to get out of here!"

He replied, "No! You're supposed to be there. These are the places where we're supposed to shine, remember?"

I had forgotten. Perhaps I was getting softer with age, along with being used to the increasingly convenient developments in other parts of China.

I adjusted my attitude and met with a former student who lived there. He was now a communist official. He listened politely as I shared the gospel with him over lunch. It didn't seem to do much good, as communists were strongly indoctrinated against religion. Nonetheless, I tried to encourage him, knowing he had a tough job. And before I left, he pulled out his phone to show me a picture he had scanned.

"Do you remember this?" he asked.

It was a picture of him, me, and Melody from 2001.

"Hey," I said, "That's great! Are you still in touch with her?"

Finally, someone said yes!

He gave me her contact info for WeChat, a Chinese version of Facebook. And that evening, Melody and I texted back and forth on our cell phones.

She brought it up: "I still remember that night on campus when we talked about Jesus. Maybe I will someday believe in God."

I told her I had been praying for her, and encouraged her to look into the Bible again.

She texted again the next day. "Can I come see you when you return to the city?" She lived about two hours away and would travel by train.

We arranged to meet at a Chinese tea room, along with another former student of mine. The other student loved the Lord, and he and I shared the gospel with Melody. Then we went out to dinner, and after the meal, Melody prayed to receive Christ as her Lord and Savior.

Better late than never!

I thought I'd never see her again. Then, 15 years later, she became a precious sister in the Lord.

Never lose hope when prayers aren't immediately answered. Sometimes it takes a while, but great testimonies are in store for those who remain faithful.

It amazes me that more than twenty years of ministry in China have passed. I would have never guessed it starting out. I was a clueless rock 'n' roller who cared only for himself. But when God, the Grace Agent, entered my life, everything changed. He turned me into one of His own grace agents, and His grace hasn't ceased to amaze me in all that He's done since.

Rockin' in the 80's at O.U.

Chapter 2

Halloween and Reformation Day

Some Christians choose not to celebrate Halloween.

I have no choice. I was born on October 31, 1965. Whether I was a trick or a treat depends on who you ask!

October 31 is also known as Reformation Day. It was the day in 1517 that Martin Luther hammered his "95 Theses" to the church door in Wittenberg. The 95 Theses challenged the then corrupt practices and teachings of the Roman Catholic Church. This sparked the Protestant Reformation.

Luther hoped to spur renewal from within, but he wasn't received kindly. However, his ideas quickly spread throughout Europe, and many united to protest and quit the established church.

They met with fierce and violent opposition. Nonetheless, the Protestant movement grew as it marked a return to the truths of Scripture that had been buried in years of corrupted tradition.

As a Christian, this means more to me than ghosts and goblins. But before I became a Christian it was a different story.

My transition from ghosts and goblins to reformation began on a Halloween weekend in 1989. I returned to my alma mater, Ohio University, to participate in its infamous Halloween celebration. Back then, my only goal in life was to have a good time.

On Friday, my friends and I hit the bars. Later in the evening, I met Tiffany.

"You look familiar," she said. "I'm sure I've seen you somewhere before."

"I graduated from here last year. Maybe you saw my rock band? I played lead guitar!" I wanted to be famous.

"That's it!" She interjected. "I organized a benefit concert you guys played. Remember?"

I did, and we hit it off. Before saying goodnight, I invited Tiffany to the Halloween party my friends were having the next evening.

The next evening we nearly missed each other. It was getting late and she hadn't yet shown up, so I left the party with another girl to watch all the antics uptown. There, we encountered thousands of dressed up "Halloweeners" parading the streets—the Mardi Gras of the Midwest!

After a while of the ridiculous revelry, we headed back to the party. Upon entering the back door, a friend called out, "Rick, someone's here looking for you."

It was Tiffany. This was a great moment for my ego, because girls were rarely interested in me. Now I had to be Mr. Smooth and get to her without the girl I was with noticing. It was a happy problem, and it happened to work out. I got to Tiffany and we picked up where we had left off.

The more the ego can be pumped, the more it can be deflated. The weekend ended, and I left O.U. feeling empty. It was now a return to life as usual. I had my fun, but the fulfillment was fleeting. At best, I could cling to the memories.

It was now back to an empty work week ahead. It seemed there was nothing to live for except the next party outing, and then the cycle would start all over again.

That week, in a desperate attempt to keep living in the past, I called Tiffany. Maybe we could pull off a long distance relationship.

Talking to her was somewhat awkward after the rush of the party weekend, and it wasn't the same on the phone. But we kept in touch, and just before Christmas, she came to Cincinnati to see me.

We went out on an official date. Although we didn't have much in common, something about her captured my heart. I wanted to continue seeing her, but Someone else began to capture *her* heart.

Each time I tried to arrange another date, she came up with some excuse. She had things to do with her family. She had to study. Then she started talking about activities with a college Christian group.

Christian group? I thought. *Where'd that come from?*

"Have you always been involved with this Christian group?" I asked.

"Not as much as now," she said, but it seemed to be getting consistent. It looked like our flirtatious fling was flying away.

I went to Ohio University again in February to take the GRE exam—a prerequisite for grad school. I contacted Tiffany, but she said she would be traveling that weekend. However, we agreed to meet on Sunday when she returned.

I wasn't sure about her any more. She had mentioned that she quit drinking, and I didn't like all the new Christian activity she was involved with. My interest began to dwindle.

On Sunday, I reluctantly stayed through the afternoon. *Why am I waiting around?* I thought. *What are we going to do together? She doesn't drink, and she seems different now.* As the day grew later, I decided to leave by 5:00 if she didn't call by then.

At 4:45, it seemed enough. I tried to go, but my car was blocked in a narrow driveway.

By the time I found who needed to move their cars, the clock struck 5:00, and the house phone rang.

What a surprise—it was Tiffany.

This was long before cell phones. If I had left I would've missed that call. As a result, we arranged to meet after dinner.

It was awkward. I met her on the college green and said, "You don't drink any more. What do you want to do?" She said she'd drink a soda if I wanted to get a beer. So we headed to a bar called The Pub.

Sitting down with no idea what to talk about, the only thing I could think was to ask, "What's all this Christian business with you lately?"

And that was it. She started beaming and talking about God and Jesus. Now I knew I lost her! I sat there blankly as she poured out enthusiasm over her return to faith. She had wandered from the faith years ago. Now she was back, and said she would live for Jesus from here on.

She then tried to persuade me.

I was very closed-minded and critical, and challenged her on several points. I had had these types of discussions before. My own mother had tried to promote God and Christian morals in our home growing up, and I was her chief antagonist.

All religions think they're right, I thought. *Nobody could really know the truth until they died. So why bother trying to figure it out?* I wasn't an atheist, I just didn't like the "rules" of Christianity. That's all it seemed to be.

When Tiffany asked me if I knew whether or not I would go to heaven, I told her, "I hope so." I thought I was a good enough person, because I never killed anybody and never stole *too much.*

Yet in this conversation, for the first time, I heard that I must be PERFECT in order to get into heaven, that I never could be, and that faith in Jesus was the ONLY way. I was told that no other religion, no matter how good, could save me. Forgiveness and reconciliation to God were available only through the blood of Jesus that was shed on the cross.

Through our discussion, it became clear that the old Tiffany was gone. She wasn't going to change. I wanted to get out of there and get home.

We left the bar and walked to her car. There, I said goodbye in a huff and rudely walked away.

When I got to my own car, I began to feel something I never felt before: shame.

It was going to be a late three hour drive from O.U. back to Cincinnati. Along the way, it dawned on me that I hadn't handled the situation well. Guilt was my passenger.

Three hours gave plenty of time to think about our discussion. *Why do people become Christians,* I thought. *What's wrong with them?* After a while of looking at them with anger, I tried to see it from their point of view. Maybe it would be nice not to desire sin. Maybe it would be nice not to "have to" drink or get high. Maybe there's a peace and satisfaction that I don't have.

But no! I love my desires. They're my life. Yet Tiffany had a noticeable glow about her. I hurled objections at her that she couldn't answer, yet she remained unmoved and glowing!

I'm happy, I thought. But again, *why do I feel guilty right now? And what about the meaning of life? Why are we here? Was this an accident? Is this all there is?* There I was, the rock 'n' roll shallow head, now pondering philosophical issues.

As the drive went on, it started to seem like there was something to what Tiffany was saying. There might be more to the Christian faith than I thought. That three hour drive drove me to serious consideration.

The next day, I told my housemate Rob about everything. Rob was a medical student at University of Cincinnati who desperately needed a place to live. No Christian in his right mind would choose to live with five other morally depraved guys like us on Glendora Avenue. Yet Rob did against all odds.

He and I went out for a beer. It put me at ease that a Christian would drink a beer with me, and we got into a meaningful conversation. I told him the whole story about what had happened, and how I was starting to get philosophical and thinking about truth. My view of the Christian faith was changing. He replied and said, "Sounds like you're on the fence, Rick."

Nervous laughter. Could it really be?

Then for the first time in my life, I owned up to the fact that I was in the wrong. I felt ashamed for how I used Tiffany and others. For the first time, I hated my impure thoughts and motives. Later I would learn that one of the first steps to becoming a Christian is the realization that you have sinned.

"Rob," I confessed, "I've acted like a real scum ball."

Rob, who seemed to be such a clean guy, surprised me with his reply. "We're ALL scum balls, Rick! That's why Christ died for us and rose again, that we might be cleansed and forgiven."

After that, I wrote Tiffany a letter and apologized for leaving the way I did. I told her I liked her, and let her know how confused she made me on the way home. "I don't know what, if anything will become of it, but you really got me thinking."

Our lives remain in Halloween darkness until Reformation Day begins to dawn.

Chapter 3

Jesus Christ Was Born Today

Maybe I still had a chance with Tiffany! I found in Rob's room a book about Christian dating and relationships. The wisdom in the book was meaningful and helpful, even though it often mentioned Jesus.

At first, I would skip over the Jesus parts. Toward the end, however, I found myself becoming more interested in Him.

The next week, Tiffany called. "I was so excited to get your letter! I'm coming to Cincinnati again. Let's meet!"

I still had a chance!

"Oh, and when I come I want you to meet my friend, Lou. Lou is a Christian, but he used to be *just like you*. I can't wait for you to meet him!"

Maybe this was no chance after all.

It sounded like an attempt to proselytize me. I didn't want that. However, by this time my curiosity was peaking. I heard my mouth agreeing to meet Lou, even though my head was thinking, *NO!*

We met at Kenwood Mall and talked for two hours. I asked all the tough questions. He answered the best he could. The difference was that this time I wasn't arguing, but inquiring.

When we finished talking, Lou gave me a little booklet entitled, "The Four Spiritual Laws." In it there was a presentation of the Gospel, and a prayer that one could say to receive Christ as Lord. I read it and wondered if I would ever take that plunge. There were still too many intellectual doubts standing between me and Christ. Did He really rise from the dead? I had to research more.

I spent the next two weeks reading apologetics books and learning about evidence that supported the resurrection of Jesus Christ. The Christian faith stood above all other religions. None of the other religions had a living Savior. No other sacred book contained fulfilled prophecies like the Bible. All other religions appeared to be man-made attempts to please God, something the Bible said couldn't be done apart from faith in Jesus.

Each night after reading, I would take out the booklet and read the prayer in the back, wondering if and when I would really mean it.

One day, so obsessed with learning the truth, I left work early with a fever. It was just a way to get home and continue reading.

That night, I needed a break. I started downstairs to get some water when my mind began to race. I was convinced that Jesus rose from the dead, and that the Christian message was true, but I was afraid of losing my life for it. I wanted to commit, but what would my friends say? What if I was wrong? What if I was right? Voices from both sides spoke on the inside as I walked down the stairs.

"Rick, you know you need to do this. Believe...take the step..."

The other voice said, "No! Are you nuts? Get back to your life now!"

The weight of the moment was more than I could handle. I knew this would be the biggest, most important decision of my life. But I hated making decisions. I hated deciding which socks to wear! This was too much. It was so overwhelming I began to cry.

This struck me, because actual tears flowed out of my eyes. Up until that point in my adult life, I had never shed a tear. At times I wanted to cry and release everything, but no matter how hard I choked up or watered, the tears never came. But they were flowing now. I felt like a baby. I went back upstairs, not wanting anyone to come home and see me like that.

Upstairs, I closed my door and sat down trembling. The voices kept whirling me about with pros and cons, and shoulds and shouldn'ts. My body shook intensely as these thoughts relentlessly troubled my head. I could find no peace or resolve.

Then, in the midst of a whirlwind of emotion and at my wits' end, I let out a spontaneous cry:

"JESUS! You win! I side with You! Come into my life!"

That was my sinner's prayer. Not quite as elegant as the one in the booklet.

Instantly, my body stopped shaking. A wave of calm flowed through me that seemed to well up from my innermost being to the outside. I didn't know what to think.

That night, Rob was the first one home. I told him what had happened, and he was elated. It was perfect timing. He had been so discouraged living in that den of depravity and was near his wits' end. This was encouragement from above.

I, on the other hand, felt unsure.

The next two days, I somewhat back-pedaled. I didn't want to give up drugs and alcohol, or humble myself to God. The world teaches us to follow our dreams and be in control of our own destiny. I kept thinking of Mel Gibson in *Lethal Weapon*, not taking orders from anybody! So the concept of humbling myself to Another was very new and hard to swallow. I was also hesitant to accept the reliability of the Bible. At this point, I hadn't even read it yet.

I had never been to church either. When Sunday came, I forced myself to go and at least check it out after all of this. "Forced" is putting it lightly. I probably had the worst headache of my life that morning, and there was no drinking the night before. But Rob woke me up, and I was committed.

The preacher preached on God's grace. This comforted me, as it addressed some of the issues I was dealing with. After the service I saw some people I actually knew, which also put me at ease. My headache went away, too!

I decided I wanted to get closer to God, but didn't yet feel like a Christian.

Rob took me to a fellowship meeting the next Tuesday, but it was more solemn and religious than I was ready for. During the prayer time, I prayed quietly, "God, I want to be who You want me to be, but it doesn't feel like I can fit in here." There was no desire to fit in, either.

That Saturday, Tiffany called. I told her I had "prayed the prayer to become a Christian."

"That's wonderful!" she said. "Why don't you come up to O.U. this weekend?"

I jumped in the car and drove up that day.

That evening, she took me to one of *her* fellowship meetings. I felt tricked. *Here we go again,* I thought on the way.

This meeting, however, was livelier, and I actually enjoyed it. I learned that different groups could have different personalities, and that I didn't have to compromise my own. It was an answer to prayer.

Driving back on Sunday gave another three hours to reflect on everything. This time, though, peace and comfort were my passengers.

A revelation came that would seal me into my new life. Driving along, I thought to myself, *could I ever go back to my old ways of thinking and live by them again?* I thought long and hard through the ride, not paying any attention to the cassette tape that was playing, songs from a rock group called Big Star. I finally concluded: *No, I don't think so.* Then I remembered someone telling me that when Jesus Christ comes into your heart, He will never leave you.

I started to laugh. It was settled. He won't leave me, and I won't leave Him. No turning back. This is who I am from here on.

The next song on the tape came on. I had forgotten that music was even playing, but now I tuned in. It wasn't a Christian album, but oddly enough, it had a Christmas song. Alex Chilton sang the words,

"Jesus Christ was born today, Jesus Christ was born."

What timing! I laughed as the song played, at that moment realizing the life of Christ had been birthed in me.

A new course for life had been set. I had no idea where it would take me, but I knew it wouldn't be with Tiffany. She fell in love and married Lou.

Chapter 4

Clueless in Cincinnati

"God has a wonderful plan for your life!"

I was told this when I first heard the gospel, and it's commonly taught. Ultimately, it's true. But not everything that happens is a part of God's wonderful plan. It's a mistake to think that everything is ordained as you travel your path. No, God's wonderful plan is that He is with you every step of the way, and that He can even work with your missteps.

His plan for my life progressed as I enrolled in a Masters' program at University of Cincinnati and studied Communication. I thought I was going into radio and television, but the program actually focused on organizational and interpersonal communication theory.

"How could you get that mixed up?" you might ask.

That's how clueless I was. Even today, symptoms of cluelessness still come up now and then. But thankfully, God works with clueless people! The school accepted me and even granted me a teaching assistantship. I taught a Public Speaking course and had to learn it as I went along.

No regrets, but the Masters' degree didn't help me land a better job. After graduation, I went through a difficult year without work and had to go back to live with my parents for several months.

During that time, I latched on to a bizarre relationship with a girl named Sandra. I met her at a Christian event and went to church with her. She was dazzlingly social while I was clueless and shy. Over time, we grew serious and often talked about marriage, but I couldn't do anything without a job.

Sandra was not what she appeared to be. There were bizarre occurrences as we dated. Prank phone calls. Items in the mail I never ordered. Talk of a threatening ex-boyfriend who I never saw. And lots of arguments. One time she even pointed a knife at me. Then she would be as sweet as a lamb. So sweet, we just had to make up.

People tried to tell me something was wrong. But Clueless Me wouldn't listen. Some singles fear losing a girlfriend or boyfriend when it would actually be in their best interest. They'd rather hope for the best in spite of all the danger signs. They fear the alternative loneliness. That was me. I convinced myself that everybody else just didn't understand.

God's wonderful plan for our lives is that we walk in the truth. The Lord was trying to bring the truth to me all along, but because of weakness, I resisted.

It took a pop on the jaw to finally wake me up.

One night outside of her dad's house, we had a spat and she started screaming at me. He misunderstood the situation and sent me away with a fist to my face! At that, I went home realizing the relationship should end.

That night, I received a bizarre call. It was Sandra, pretending to be child. She worked with kids and tried to make me think this was one of them. I wondered if she had multiple personalities or something.

Shocked and shaken, I went to see my friend Barry Lloyd, who was experienced in counseling. He said it was a classic description of borderline personality disorder. He confirmed that the relationship should end and prepared me for the varying responses that were to come. She would not let me go easily.

For several days, everything Barry said happened. Meanwhile, I progressively learned of lies she had been telling, not only to me, but also ABOUT me. The Lord brought it all out in the open. I even became friends with a couple who initially hated me because of what they'd heard. God revealed the truth to them and vindicated me.

That couple, myself, and others tried talking to Sandra about getting help. She didn't seem to listen at the time, but she didn't get angry about it. She eventually moved to another State and got married. I hope all is well.

As the dust settled, I got a temporary job and moved in with Barry, who lived far away from the city. It felt like being exiled in the wilderness, but I drew closer to the Lord. I started devouring spiritual books. I continued to look for a real job, but stopped stressing out. It wasn't easy, but I learned to say, "This is the day that the Lord has made. I will rejoice and be glad in it."

Sometimes God's wonderful plan doesn't work out so quickly, because we're clueless. God sees something that we miss. He's either preparing us or sparing us. We may not yet be ready for the good that's coming. Or, he has better in store for us.

If I had gotten a good job while dating Sandra, I would have bought the ring. Going without work was a great trial, but being trapped in a disastrous marriage would have been worse. The Lord kept and protected me through it all. And through it all, Clueless Me became a little wiser!

Chapter 5

Introduction to Missions

God doesn't bring all the troubles into our lives, but God "works all things for good to those who love Him" (Romans 8:28). That means when some of the "all things" in life are unpleasant, God can redeem them. One of the blessings that resulted from the Sandra episode was that I connected with Faith Bible Church in Cincinnati. They became like family. And it didn't take long before this missions-minded church had me doing a week of ministry in Mexico.

Some people debate the effectiveness of short-term missions. I've seen lasting fruit in China because of short-term missionaries. And my first mission trip was only a week long, but packed with the power of God.

In August, 1992, we arrived at a Tijuana ministry site that camped several teams from other churches. We all worshiped together in the mornings and went out to minister in the afternoons. We took bucket showers and used out-houses. Our team captured a tarantula and kept it in a jar.

In the village of Los Flores, a woman allowed us to use her home for outreach. Daily we would invite people to come and see what we were doing. Some of the group worked with children. Others held Bible studies, and some played sports with the teens. Then we preached in the evenings. That week, 36 people prayed to receive Christ as their Lord and Savior!

Four teenage boys were reached through the sports ministry early in the week. They were so excited about their new life in Christ, they helped us invite others to come the rest of the week.

One of the boys was extremely bold in his witnessing to the neighbors. One night, time was running out, but he wanted to knock on one more door. It was late, but he insisted he *had to* invite this last person.

The invited man came to the evening service. Before we even started, he walked to the front and asked if he could pray to receive Jesus!

"All day long I've felt like I had to do this," he said.

The Holy Spirit was really the One doing the inviting. One lady kept making excuses, but she finally showed up and gave her life to the Lord.

"I couldn't resist anymore," she said.

The most touching moment came on the last night. Pedro was the husband of Theresa, the lady who let us use her home. Earlier in the week, she had told us that Pedro used to beat her and forbid her to practice her Christian faith. When they moved to Los Flores, he gave in and allowed her to gradually start doing things. Pedro attended each night's service, observing everything from the back. On the last night, however, he came forward and said yes to God. When he went over to hug his wife, there wasn't a dry eye in the place.

Frequently the people told us they were overwhelmed. "You came such a long way from your homes to share the good news with us." We were told we had given them everything.

What an amazing introduction to missions!

And yet, that was good enough for me. I wasn't interested in going anywhere else. In fact, I got tired of all the emphasis that Faith Bible Church placed on missions. Even the young adult group often expressed interest in missionary activity.

Sometimes I felt awkward, thinking, *why don't I care as much as they do?*

One evening the group was out eating pizza. Someone started the conversation with, "If you were going to be a missionary, which country would you want to go to?" As others around the table exuberantly shared where they desired to go, I hoped no one would ask me. I didn't want to go anywhere. Finally they did ask me, and I told them just that.

"But if you HAD to choose somewhere, where would it be?" they pressed.

"I don't know," I said. But grasping for anything, I uttered, "Maybe China."

Chapter 6

Tipping the Scales

We all face decisions every day. Some are obviously weightier than others. What do you do when you don't know what to do?

As things got better in Cincinnati, I debated whether or not to go to seminary. I still had no job, and the prospect of going into full time Bible study was compelling.

I later learned that some seminaries will actually take the fun out of Bible study and kill your faith. But I applied and got accepted to a school near Chicago.

After praying about it, I couldn't sense God's will in the matter. And I didn't sense any clear calling to be a pastor or teacher after seminary. On the other hand, I didn't sense God saying no. I could've argued that He'd eventually call me if I took a step of faith and went.

With the deadline approaching, Pastor Keith Missel gave me valuable advice. "When it's difficult to make a decision because either side could be argued well, look for the 1% that outweighs the other side. Then just go with that!"

That was helpful, because I was looking for a strong case to base my decision on.

The Lord doesn't hide His will like a puzzle. If it's not clear, wait until it is clear. But if a decision is required before that, find the 1% that tips the scales!

I found my 1%. Although there was a desire to go, I didn't sense a clear calling in the matter. Because of that, I couldn't justify going into debt to pay for school. Back to looking for a job.

The day after committing this decision to God, one of Cincinnati's biggest companies called me in for an interview. I couldn't believe it. I had dropped off a resume there thinking, *that's a company that will never hire me.*

The interview process went surprisingly well. I got the job, and a grueling season of my life had ended.

It took a while, but God came through big in the end. Sometimes we have to wait. But even during that time He's coming through in ways we may fail to appreciate.

If you're in a stressful season, be encouraged that it will pass. The scales will tip in your favor. In the meantime, concentrate on what's good.

The job was intense. A poorly planned organizational move in the company resulted in all kinds of operational and corporate blunders. While calls piled up in my voicemail, messages piled up on my desk. Mail and faxes needed urgent response. The daily routine consisted of putting out fires, dealing with angry people on the phone, and coming up with answers that I didn't have.

It was nuts for four months before the work calmed down. But it went fast.

When everything settled, I had more time to remember that I was a bachelor. At that time, God didn't give me a wife, but gave me a close friend in Don Trevis. We connected at Faith Bible Church and discovered a kindred spirit.

We started off criticizing a lot going on with the church. We probably sinned greatly as we talked for hours in what might be called, *sanctified gossip*. That's when you criticize folks or situations under a guise of spiritual concern. Often it's just a cover for spiritual pride, and I had plenty of that.

Nonetheless, we did care, and one day we realized we had been doing too much talking and not enough praying! We started praying for the church and watched God answer the concerns that were on our hearts.

Within two years, the job became unfulfilling. Instead of pursuing a promotion or a different position, all I could think about was going into ministry. More decisions needed to be made.

I didn't have to look for the 1% to tip the scales. The desire to go into ministry was strong. It was just a question of what that meant and how to follow through.

Chapter 7

Music or Missions

I wanted to be a rock star.

In my college days I played lead guitar in bands that played everything from pop to punk. After becoming a Christian, I found a group of guys just across the river in Kentucky. We aspired to succeed in Christian rock, and we practiced in lead singer Mark Kinman's church.

Practice never made perfect. We lacked unity. The bassist and the drummer were sometimes unreliable. Nonetheless, we did have fun jamming at times, and Mark and I became close friends. We both had a missions mindset.

The Lord started fueling that mindset. One night, I invited the band to my apartment and showed them a videotaped sermon from a popular missions conference. In it, the preacher declared, "America is overstaffed! Go someplace where you're really needed!"

"What do you think about this?" I asked the group.

Mark said something like, "Makes you stop and think, doesn't it?"

No reaction from the others.

But the message haunted me. It challenged comfortable living and excessive consumerism. Wish I didn't hear it before going on a vacation the next week!

At that time, I read voraciously. No fluff for me. I filled up on "no compromise" authors like A.W. Tozer, A.B. Simpson, and the Puritans.

Oh, the Puritans! It was like mining pure gold, because they were so devotional. They could communicate the grace and glory of God better in one paragraph than modern authors could do in entire books! Yet, years later, I would discover they laid a foundation for bondage and legalism in my life. God eventually set me free and gave me a total paradigm shift. More about that later. Nonetheless, I devoured the classics and often wanted to get away from people just so I could get alone with my books.

As I continued to practice with a band that was going nowhere, I began to question my motives in life and what I was really after. That missions video impacted me, but a tract from Keith Green practically changed my course.

Keith Green was a popular Christian singer from the 70's. I was more of a hard rocker, but still enjoyed his then contemporary style. What appealed to me was that he preached a no compromise message. In fact, he was more about the message than the music. He used his music only as a platform to preach the gospel and challenge the church.

He and his wife, Melody, started Last Days Ministries near Lindale, Texas. Last Days was a community where people came to live, work, and study the Bible together. They published a magazine and many tracts, all in a very creative manner that appealed to multitudes of young people.

In his tract, "Music or Missions," Keith showed how misguided it was to give so much esteem and applause to rock stars, while missionaries who sacrifice all for the Lord are hardly thought of. He wrote,

"Today, so many people ask me if I can tell them how they can start or enter into a music ministry. At concerts I get countless questions about this, and I also get lots of letters and even some long-distance phone calls from many people who feel they are only 'called' into the music ministry. One day I began to ask myself why so few have ever asked me how to become a missionary, or even a local street preacher, or how to disciple a new believer. It seems everyone would prefer the 'bright lights' of what they think a music ministry would be, rather than the mud and obscurity of the mission field, or the streets of the ghetto, or even the true spiritual sweetness of just being a nobody whom the Lord uses mightily in small 'everyday' ways."

The tract challenged readers to live more for the applause of the Lord than for the applause of man.

At the same time, a Christian Rock magazine had been coming in the mail. Strangely enough, I never ordered it! But I read it and learned a lot. Some musicians seemed to be in it for the ministry, but many talked more about making a living. It was all about the money. And some of the artists were only doing Christian because they couldn't get secular contracts.

The Lord was opening my eyes. My band played on, but the dream of being a rock star began to fizzle.

It was time to investigate different ministry options.

One option was to serve with an inner city ministry in Chicago. I was drawn to this place because it was the home of a Christian band that played hard rock. They also preached a no compromise message. Maybe I could serve the Lord AND play guitar with them!

They were hippies from the 70's, and Don Trevis and I spent a night in their commune. We checked out their soup-kitchen ministry and attended their inner city church service. At the commune, we talked to several residents about how they got there and what they were doing. We laughed at a large rat running from the kitchen to the first floor bathroom.

The whole experience was eye opening. It seemed like everyone in the commune was stuck there. No one we talked to had any vision for what could come next. I was looking for a launching board, not a final destination, so this wasn't the place for me.

Keith Green died in a plane wreck in 1982, but his legacy continued through his recordings and writings. One night I finished a book of his sermons. The pages in the back of the book had pictures and information for Last Days Ministries. All I did was flip through them, and I KNEW this was the place to go. I didn't even have to go to Texas to check it out first. I just started the communication process and applied for the program.

The program was called a Discipleship Training School. It was connected with a larger mission organization called YWAM. The program consisted of three months' work and study at the ministry and then a two month mission outreach. It would expose me to different ministry opportunities as well as missions. Maybe I could play guitar with their musicians as well!

Of course, I flip-flopped on whether I would really go through with it. It meant quitting my job and moving out of my cool apartment. It meant leaving family and friends to go off into the great unknown.

I submitted my fears to God. I prayed, "What about my future? How will I support a family later? Should I really leave a decent paying job?"

The Lord then gave me Psalm 37:25:

> "I have been young, and now am old; yet I have not seen the righteous forsaken, nor his descendants begging bread" (NKJV).

That scripture penetrated the depths of my inner man and gave me the courage to move forward in faith. I would not be forsaken. My future wife and kids would always have what they need, because the LORD is our provider. And as long as the Psalmist David had lived, he'd never seen it otherwise with God's righteous ones.

It's still true today. You may be thinking, "Yeah, but I don't qualify. I'm not righteous enough." If you have placed your faith in Jesus Christ, you are righteous. It's not your righteousness, but HIS. It's a free gift through the shed blood and perfect obedience of Jesus. It is a righteousness by faith, a gift of God, and not of your own works. You will never be forsaken.

On March 11, 1994, I wrote in my journal,

> At press time, I plan to quit my job, walk out on faith, go to Texas and join forces with YWAM for five months. After that, hopefully a longer term doing missions work. I can't believe I'm writing this.

Chapter 8

Faith Under Fire

Big moves are never easy. As my departure date in September 1994 approached, I began to waver about leaving friends and family behind. I was actively involved with a small group, a nursing home ministry, two inner city missions, and worked with fatherless kids. They needed male role models, and it wasn't like there were lines of volunteers waiting to come and help.

Later, however, I discovered that while I was wondering if God wanted me to stay for those kids' sake, He was actually waiting for me to leave! Shortly after I left, God brought in someone better with kids than I ever was.

Discouragement knocked hard at the door. In all that I was involved with, I hadn't seen much fruit. In fact, folks who seemed to be making progress had a relapse. Friends and family members that I loved hadn't responded to the gospel. And I felt helpless as a friend went through a severe trial. Hardly encouraging when you're pursuing full time ministry.

Yet God showed me that faith must be exercised when all else would suggest otherwise. Faith is easy when things are going well. Faith is easy when you understand the situation. Faith is easy when others are with you.

But the Bible reveals a different type of faith. It reveals a faith based not on what we see (2Corinthians 4:16-18) or understand (Proverbs 3:5). It reveals a faith that believes, in spite of hopeless situations (Romans 4:18). It records the faithful ones who triumphed against all odds, and those who even stood in the face of torture (Hebrews 11). It teaches a faith that can be joyful in spite of trials (James 1:2). And above all, it reveals Jesus, "the author and finisher of our faith, who for the joy set before him endured the cross, despising the shame, and has sat down at the right hand of the throne of God" (Heb. 12:2).

Hallelujah! Jesus overcame. "And this is the victory that overcometh the world, even our faith" (1John 5:4; KJV). Victory doesn't come through easy living. It comes through perseverance. The good news is that the outcome is already in our favor. The trials will pass. The rewards await.

Five days to go, and saying goodbye to people was much harder than expected. On the plus side, I got to share the gospel with many as I tried to explain where I was going.

On the downside, my parents thought I was leaving for a cult. I assured them that I wasn't moving to a cult site, but they weren't thoroughly convinced. They also brought up money matters.

"What will you do at the end of the 5 months?"

"I don't know yet."

With that uncertainty, I moved all of my stuff into their basement. They were ultimately supportive of me even though they didn't fully understand.

Just before leaving, I wrote in my journal,

> Everyone is watching. My family is watching. My unbelieving relatives are watching. My former workmates are watching. My friends, the church, everybody's watching. What will God do with this Rick person next? Stay tuned...

And out the door I went! I flew to Texas, fighting the nerves and realizing I had just left life as I knew it.

A brother from the ministry met me at the airport.

"There's not much out where we are," he said as he drove me to the ministry base, "except rattlesnakes, spiders, and chiggers. Oh, we also find scorpions here and there! But you really have to watch out for the brown recluse spiders. They're everywhere."

We arrived at the base, which was secluded about ten miles away from any kind of city life. I kept reassuring myself, "This isn't a cult. This isn't a cult!" Then somebody greeted us and took me to the room I would be sharing with four other guys. So much for the privacy I had known and cherished. This was going to require some adjusting.

As I put sheets on my upper bunk bed, I searched the mattress for spiders.

Chapter 9

What Have I Done?

Last Days Ministries was a charismatic group that drew believers from all kinds of churches, both traditional and lively. Off and on I heard different terms and expressions from other students and wondered if we were all on the same page.

Culture shock hit hard, going from my quiet single apartment to sharing a noisy dorm with guys of different ages. I felt trapped not having a car there and didn't adjust to the changes well. The devil took advantage of this and started me thinking, *what have I gotten myself into?*

But God is faithful. I managed to get alone with Him and found comfort in Psalm 91.

> He who dwells in the secret place of the Most High shall abide under the shadow of the Almighty. I will

say of the LORD, He is my refuge and my fortress, my God. In Him I will trust (vs.1-2).

It reminded me to dwell in the safety of the secret place. That's the place of God's unseen presence and love. I was dwelling too much on the circumstances at hand. Sometimes we need a perspective shift.

The next day was Sunday. I skipped church because I wanted to take advantage of an empty dorm and have more quiet time with the Lord. He met with me, even as a church skipper. The peace started to come. I also made friends with some other church skippers.

Still, the first days at Last Days had me up and down.

Coming from a more traditional background, I struggled with some of the teaching in the first sessions. As a new believer, I had read books that taught me to look suspiciously at any brand of Christianity that didn't express things in the most conservative and orthodox expressions. These "heresy hunters" basically conditioned me to hunt for heresies myself, rather than to hear what God might be saying through imperfect preachers.

In many cases, "heresy hunters" throw out the baby with the bathwater. They nitpick and focus on what they disagree with while ignoring anything that's good. There's a place for scrutiny in the church, but it has often been unfair and overdone.

I'm ashamed that I wasn't stronger, but in the middle of all the faith around me, I began to have doubts. *Maybe God didn't want me here, after all,* I thought.

I got on the dorm phone and called two friends back home, hoping they would each give me a green light to come back.

"Do you really think you made a mistake after the last six months of praying and preparing to be there?"

Well, that wasn't exactly a green light.

"I wouldn't make any hasty decisions," said the other. "Proverbs 21:5 says that haste leads to poverty."

No green light there either. Maybe yellow, though. He suggested I talk about my concerns with someone first and then give it two weeks. Then at least people wouldn't be surprised by a sudden departure. So I went and talked with one of the staff.

"We've seen people come into the school with the same kind of apprehension," he said, "and they ended up loving it!"

I didn't doubt that, but I was skeptical that it would be me.

Within days, however, I started to appreciate the teaching sessions more. One man taught about the love of God in a way I had never considered before. It was so much more than a fluffy greeting card type of love, or what some people humorously call, "sloppy agape." It made me want to live all-out for Jesus. It's the goodness of God that leads to repentance (Romans 2:4), and the love of Christ compels us (2Corinthians 5:14). We get messed up when obedience results only from a sense of duty or guilt. Love is the empowering force of the Christian life.

In time I had to repent for not being very loving, and realized that I was something of a charisphobic. I withdrew from some of the more charismatic brothers and sisters because I felt threatened by their differences and skeptical of their experiences. That's just a nice way to say I was prejudiced and not willing to come down from my superior throne! God opened my eyes to see that no single church or denomination has a corner on truth. I also started to appreciate the beautiful unity through diversity within the body of Christ.

I'll finish out the time here, I plotted, but thought about skipping the mission trip at the end. I really missed everyone back home. I wrote in my journal, "When I get home I want to tell everybody I love them and just enjoy being in their midst—and they'll probably think I've just returned from a cult!"

Chapter 10

The Winds of Heaven Blow

"It's time for us to discuss the mission trip options that are available," the leaders announced. "This year we have four choices."

Surely one of them would be Mexico. It's so close to Texas! Because of that, I had already brushed up on my Spanish before coming to the school.

"This year the choices are Russia, South Africa, China, or a Native-American reservation. Take a week to pray about it, and then let us know where you want to go."

¿Qué? What happened to Mexico?

The staff then discussed the plans for each trip. When they talked about China, I knew that's where I was headed. But I didn't want to go there. I had read about Chinese Christians imprisoned for their faith. It was a communist country, and it was so far away! I didn't even know how to use chopsticks! But I couldn't shake the sense that I needed to choose China.

Praying through each option, I hoped to hear from the Lord differently. Then one of my friends approached me.

"Rick! Why don't you choose South Africa? That's where I'm going. It will be amazing!"

"Yeah," I answered, "we'd have a great time together!"

That seemed to settle it. But before I walked away, I felt compelled to say, "No. I'd like to, but I think the Lord wants me to go to China."

That week, the dorm buzzed with talk about the mission trips. I started to second guess again. Maybe I would just skip the trip and move back home to other things. Don Trevis wrote me a letter suggesting we do ministry together when I return. I was almost ready to leave then.

But one afternoon, I found a quiet place to pray. Not only did China seem to be the Lord's will, it seemed He was calling me to more than just six weeks there. That didn't thrill me, but I couldn't argue with Him. I had no excuses. I wanted to say, "I have to pay off my debts." But they were already paid off. I wanted to say, "I have responsibilities here in America." But I had no pressing responsibilities. There was no reason whatsoever to stick around.

A recent class on missions played back in my mind. That week we were stirred as the teacher went through Old and New Testament passages revealing God's desire to bless all nations. It wasn't just the Great Commission found in Matthew 28:18-20. It began in the book of Genesis with the blessing of Abraham, who would become a father of many nations. It continued throughout the Bible, as God sought to bring salvation through the Jews, which culminated in the Messiah. It ends with all nations worshiping before the throne in the book of Revelation.

The entire Bible reveals God's heart for the world. He is pleased when sinners repent. Therefore, missions should be an act of worship, fueled not just by a love for souls, but by a desire to bless the Lord.

He came to seek and save the lost. When we do the same, we are in sync with Him.

Then the teaching on the love of God played back in my mind. Two scriptures were highlighted:

> The LORD thy God in the midst of thee is mighty; he will save, he will rejoice over thee with joy; he will rest in his love, he will joy over thee with singing. (Zephaniah 3:17; KJV).

And,

For the LORD takes pleasure in His people...(Psalm 149:4).

I thought about all my striving to please God, when all the while He was already pleased. It's easier to mistakenly think that God's disappointed and just tolerating us. But because of Christ, He sees us differently.

The love of God is not just a general concept to be realized in a future age. It is present and active in the here and now.

As I entered into prayer, I believed He was rejoicing over me then and there. *He was even singing.* Not because I was worthy, but because His word said so.

Then the presence of the Holy Spirit came upon me in such a powerful manner that I slumped in my chair and tears began to flow. It seemed like heaven opened up in that room, and all I could do was thank Him and worship.

In the wind of the Holy Spirit, going to China would be a breeze! "No problem, Lord. I can go to China for however long you want. I can go ANYWHERE if you go with me!" His presence was the key. It opened my heart, and I came out of that room filled and ready to go.

When the wind blows, the cradle will rock. When the Holy Spirit fills a Christian, He rocks our world. But it's in a good way. It becomes easy to move for the Lord, whether that means going overseas or simply living a holy life. Obedience is the fruit of God's love, not the cause. Things are difficult when we feel we have to prove ourselves in order to get Him to smile. But that's religion, not the gospel.

The good news is that God is mighty to save, and then He RESTS in His love (Zephaniah 3:17). Because of Jesus, He's not waiting for us to measure up. He's pleased with faith (Heb. 11:6). Believing He rejoices over you with singing will change your life.

Before we ever cared or tried to do anything for Him, Jesus died for us. He saw value in us even in our worst condition. Now being born again, how much greater His love! Yet many Christians struggle because they think of God as only *tolerating* them. Few think of Him as rejoicing over them with GLADNESS. They understand the grace that saves, but they don't understand the grace that smiles.

The wind continued to blow. One morning the dorm phone rang at 7:30 a.m. Keith Missel was on the line and asked me what my plans were for the missions outreach. I told him about China, and he replied that our church was planning a missions banquet. They chose my trip as one of the projects to raise funds for. The money started coming in, and I didn't even have to ask!

Not only was the Lord bringing things together for the trip, but He was working in another area.

Jennifer Sanford had spent a year and a half as a missionary in China. She came home to America thinking a master's degree could help her stay long term in China. Instead, she was led to Last Days Ministries. She never got her master's degree, but she ended up marrying me—and I already had one. That degree hadn't done anything for me in America, but it turned out to be invaluable in China.

My first encounter with Jennifer was in a food line. We argued. I thought I knew better how to reach the Chinese because of reading about the great missionary, Hudson Taylor. Never mind that she had already lived there. She knew more about Hudson Taylor, too. It's a wonder she even continued to talk to me!

At another time, I had a dream that was more like a vision. Her face appeared to hover before me. There was no interaction or anything. I was simply drawn to the beauty of her face. The dream had me wondering in the morning, but after that I thought nothing more about it. Life went on.

Then one day we ran into each other outside with some mutual friends.

"I've heard people say that you're funny," she challenged.

I told her to wait a minute and ran into the dorm. I returned wearing a T-shirt that said, "SPAM."

"How's this?" I asked.

Spam was originally a processed meat and was pretty funny back in the day. I probably charmed her with some one-liners as well. The important thing was that she laughed, and that made us friends.

She also had a car and offered me rides to Walmart. We saw each other around the campus and sometimes ate together. But I didn't want to get my hopes up.

One night I told the Lord that I wasn't going to pursue her. If we were to continue seeing each other, it would have to be in the ordinary scheme of things. I wouldn't go out of my way looking for her. The next day, however, our paths crossed, and we started to grow closer.

We had to be careful because she knew she wanted to stay in China after the group trip. I planned to come back home and work for a year before making the big move to China. I envisioned writing letters to her during that time.

But it didn't turn out that way.

The team going to China was fairly large, so the leaders divided us into two groups. One would go to Beijing and the other would go to a smaller city, Liaocheng. Jennifer was assigned to the team and place that I wasn't. I accepted it as God's will, offered her a handshake and said, "It's been fun. Maybe we can get in touch after the trip and meet again in the future."

A few days later, a special meeting was called for both teams. One of the leaders spoke up, "We've been checking into things, and it looks like *we can all go as one group again* and go to both places in China TOGETHER." Several students expressed enthusiasm about this change, but I think I was the happiest.

The winds of heaven were blowing in my favor. And the Lord continued to stir my heart about a long term commitment to China. I wrote in my journal,

> Chasing after God. I believe there's no greater way to run after Him than to give myself to His greatest desire: to reach unreached peoples. With Christ as my life, I cannot be fulfilled in building up what I was once after, the American Dream. Jesus has more to offer and more worth than anything else.
>
> As He left His home to bring revelation of Himself to a world that didn't know, so must I follow His lead and bring the gospel to those who have not heard...

The end won't come until all nations have heard. So why are we wasting time? I'm able to go. If God continues to provide and open the doors, I'm there.

God continued to provide and open the doors. When I told my plans to one day go back to China long term, some of the leaders said, "Why don't you just stay there after your group leaves?"

That threw me for a loop. It was too short of notice! Yet it all worked out. Jennifer was going to stay and go back to Kunming where she had lived before. She could connect me with the international school there, and I could teach. Once again, I had no excuse not to do it.

Chapter 11

Citizens From Another World

We flew into Beijing on January 7, 1995. It looked like a Chinatown from one of our major cities, only on a much larger scale. Almost every sign had Chinese characters without a speck of English. When English did appear, it was misspelled or translated incorrectly. A sea of bicycles on the side of the road outnumbered the cars, and the traffic was chaotic. Horns continually sounded as vehicles and pedestrians just missed hitting each other. It was all business as usual, and not a look of emotion showed on anyone's face!

Everybody dressed the same. We westerners were now the foreigners, and you could spot us a mile away. This made us the objects of much attention. Jennifer and I could go into a small shop to buy a soda, and a large crowd would gather to watch. Children would point, giggle and shout the only English word they knew, "HELLO!" and shout it again and again.

After a couple of days we headed for Liaocheng, located in Shandong province. It took an eight hour train and a three hour bus ride to get there. We stayed on a college campus, took some culture classes and made friends with the students and faculty.

It seemed like living in the past. Donkeys pulled carts, and three-wheeled bicycles carried loads of goods, sometimes piled quite high. The streets were dirty and the air was dusty. People burned coal to keep warm in the winter. Many had the bad habit of hacking up phlegm, starting with a monstrous throat noise and ending with a gusher of spit. It didn't matter whether it was outdoors or indoors! Mice ran across the tattered carpet in our living quarters, and no one seemed to care. We thought they were cute.

The college fed us well. Every meal was like a banquet. The only challenge, besides learning how to use chopsticks, was that they didn't provide cold drinking water—only boiled water or hot loose leaf tea. Cold drinks weren't available anywhere. I often settled for a lukewarm soda from a street vendor outside.

It was easy to fall in love with the people. They were friendly and fun to talk with. When I entered a classroom and interacted with the students, I knew the classroom was where I belonged.

When it was time to return to Beijing, we boarded a bus that was supposed to take 10 hours to get there. *It took 25!* The bus broke down twice along the way, taking an hour and a half to fix each time. Once we got to Beijing, the drivers kept getting lost and asking directions. As small-towners stuck in a big city, they didn't know what they were doing and grew increasingly frustrated.

We were supposed to stay at a university and finally arrived at midnight, only to learn that it was the wrong one! The bus wandered again through the city to search some more and eventually stopped at a hotel around 2:00 a.m.

We waited in desperation as our hosts went in to check for rooms. It turned out there were plenty of rooms, but only the drivers and our hosts could stay in them. Few hotels were allowed to house foreigners, and this wasn't one of them. So it meant camping in the bus. It was incredibly cold, but at least we had sleeping bags.

I sat next to Jennifer for 25 hours and was thankful that we still liked each other after it was over.

After a chilling evening (no pun intended), we arrived at the correct university later that morning. The school had no program for us. We just interacted with students and spent time seeing sites in Beijing.

Jennifer and I left the Last Days team in February. We flew to Kunming, where fellow missionaries arranged housing for each of us.

I got sick with strep throat. The city seemed dirtier and the people seemed less friendly. That was how the devil welcomed me to my new home.

For two weeks everything seemed negative. Day after day, I'd hear something else about crime, corruption, or oppression, and really sense the darkness. I got more cold stares than friendly 'hellos' from the Chinese. Feeling lousy, I thought, *do I really want to stay here?*

Eventually, people began to seem friendly again. The sense of darkness and oppression lifted. The Lord seemed to be saying, "It was necessary for you to be exposed to the darkness, so you wouldn't be ignorant of it while loving the people." I only felt some of the weight the Chinese were under. It was much worse for them.

Jennifer and I were housed in apartments across town from each other. We both went to work at the international school, which at the time was just a home grown enterprise, serving a few foreign families in Kunming. Today it is one of the city's major institutions, with hundreds of students.

The marriage bug eventually bit. Jennifer said yes, and we planned to return home for the summer to get married in Mississippi.

The time intensified. I prepared lessons, looked for college jobs, studied Chinese, wondered if my mail was reaching home, bicycled across town to work, and watched my money drain fast. All of that while trying to adjust to a foreign culture at the same time. It was also overwhelming to think of the tremendous population of lost souls everywhere.

On top of that I had been reading Puritan books and becoming more aware of my faults and failures. As a result, I became increasingly aware of all the faults and failures within the church. It didn't make for a joyful Christian.

That's what happens when we don't have grace for ourselves. We become more judgmental of others, because it makes us feel better about our own faults. Also, since I thought God was frowning on all my shortcomings, I thought I was taking "a holy stance" if I frowned on others. How quickly I lost sight of God rejoicing over me!

The gospel is about what Jesus did, not about how we measure up. Judgment and criticism may produce some outward change, but it usually doesn't last. It's God's goodness through grace (not nitpicking) that leads to real heart change (Romans 2:4).

Even though I was getting more introspective about sin, I still understood that God loved me. Before leaving for America in June, I knew that this entire experience had changed me. The future was unclear, but God's love would see me through. I wrote,

> In about two weeks I'll be returning to America. I wanted to say, "I'll be going home," but then the Bible says that our citizenship is in heaven. I'm sure I will not seem the same to my family and friends. I'm challenged as to what I'm really doing with my life and not knowing what the future holds. I need to be steadfast and not worry about making mistakes. The Lord's love is unfailing. He is the Great Shepherd, and His plans are to prosper us and not harm us (Jeremiah 29:11).What is trust? I must do that.

Becoming aware of sins and failures has its place, but it's better to trust in Jesus. It's better to concentrate on God's finished work in Christ than to try doing better. God's love transforms us. The more we trust in His love, as opposed to our works, the more powerfully we are changed. It makes us become like foreigners wherever we are in this world. We end up doing things differently and seeing things differently, like an American in China.

Chapter 12

God's Got You Covered

Culture shock is the feeling of disorientation that one experiences when placed in a cultural environment different from what they're used to. Oddly enough, I experienced little to none in China. However, *reverse culture shock* hit when we returned to America after only five months of being away.

The multitude of shopping choices was overwhelming. I stood stumped in Walmart's shampoo aisle. In China, only one or two choices were available back then.

It was also humbling to come home and not be noticed. In China, everywhere we went produced stares and smiles. It was like being a celebrity. Here, nobody cared. But it was great to be back and to understand everyone in our own language.

The frantic schedule began. There were churches to speak at, friends to see, and preparations to make before returning to China. I answered 1001 questions about our upcoming wedding. The plan was to leave for China two weeks after the wedding, and then I would teach at a college that had just offered a job.

However, a letter came stating that the job offer had been cancelled. That was troubling. I was counting on the school's income to help with some financial support.

It seemed like a bad deal, but it turned out to be good. God makes "all things work together for good to those who love God, to those who are the called according to His purpose" (Romans 8:28).

Later in Kunming, I met the older missionary who got the job instead. She met with our home church group regularly and revealed a lot about the school. Besides loading her down with teaching responsibilities, they mistreated her, invaded her privacy, and subjected her to many unreasonable demands. It was a blessing that I never worked there.

Our wedding took place in Mississippi. We had a honeymoon in Gatlinburg, and then three days in Cincinnati to accomplish five days' worth of tasks. The stress didn't help our already stressed relationship.

Talk about culture shock, Jennifer and I had *marriage shock*. We were two very independent people who found it difficult to adjust to being husband and wife. Let's just say we clashed.

It probably wasn't the best decision to go back to the mission field so quickly. But as we sat on the plane, I gave it all to God. Because of Jesus, no situation is beyond hope.

We took off. Twenty hours later, we landed in Kunming with luggage full of two years' worth of goods we couldn't buy in Asia.

It was fun setting up house at Jennifer's old apartment. However, it was hard to be married. I kept feeling like I wanted to go home, but then realized *I was* home! We would get into arguments and there would be no place for either of us to go cool down. If we walked out of our tiny dwelling, we found ourselves in the midst of stares from the Chinese people. They were everywhere. And when they saw us they would sincerely or mockingly call out in the only English they knew, "HELLO!" Either way, we wanted to respond like Christians.

But I didn't feel like a Christian. All the recent life changes had gotten to me. And the devil hammered me continuously. "If you were a real Christian, you would do better!" "Why don't you just quit?" "How can God ever use you?"

One night, terrible thoughts assaulted my mind. Tempted to despair, I thought, *how can I be a true Christian and think like that?* But then a light came on inside. It became clear that these evil thoughts didn't originate with me. I was being played by demonic suggestions. It was time to fight back. In this case, I literally shooed invisible demons away from my ears and said, "I rebuke you in the name of Jesus!"

We get into trouble when we take ownership of any and every thought that pops into mind. If something is contrary to God's Word, don't entertain it. Pop it back out.

Though I was learning how to recognize the enemy, I still didn't like what I saw in myself. Marital problems ensued, and so much selfishness rose to the surface.

Still a rocker, I vented out some frustration by writing a song. The words are satirical, to show the ugly nature of selfish love:

I React © October 1995

I'll scratch your back and you scratch mine
If you meet my needs everything will be fine
Say the right words, put on the right show
And I'll be the right man and our love will grow
But if you make a mistake, if you seem to neglect
I'll pull back my love and everything will be wrecked

Because I react, I'm a reactor
My love's so unstable such a delicate factor
Press all the wrong buttons and you'll get a disaster
Because I react, I'm a reactor

I've given you the right to satisfy my needs
I'll take all your flowers but I don't want your weeds
To hold a grudge is so wrong, to forgive is divine
Be sure to remember when it comes to faults of mine
And I'll be so happy if you do as you should
If you want my love to last then you better be good

Because I react, I'm a reactor...

The song was funny but too close to home. God's love is completely different. He gave His best for us when we were His enemies. His love wasn't reactive but *proactive*. Marriage is a place to practice God's kind of love. But I was so immature and without understanding.

Feeling like a failure and a hypocrite, it seemed that God had to be angry with all my recent screw-ups. The only thing I did right was stay in the Word and keep on reading, in spite of feelings of unworthiness.

Then one night I had a major revelation while reading the book of Romans.

"Therefore, having been justified by faith, we have peace with God through our Lord Jesus Christ" (Romans 5:1).

It was a familiar verse, but this time it seemed to jump off the page. Those words, "PEACE WITH GOD" arrested me. It was as if the Holy Spirit grabbed my head and forced me to look at the following words, "through our Lord Jesus Christ."

Or, in other words, *through Jesus, not through Rick's performance.*

Could it be? Was everything well between God and me, in spite of all my recent thoughts and actions? Was peace possible?

Yes! Because it didn't depend on me. Peace with God came through JESUS, because HE paid for my sins. Why did I start to think I could detract from that? Why did I think I had to earn that peace by being good?

The burden was removed. I no longer feared the Lord would ditch me after every mess up with Jennifer.

That didn't give me a license to be a jerk. But as my relationship with God grew, things got better with us. It probably took two years before we were comfortable with being married. And we still have our challenges today, but we have since enjoyed many happy years together.

Meanwhile, I taught seven different English classes at a Chinese high school. Between getting in arguments with Jennifer and shouting above the noise of more than 60 students per class, I got tired and hoarse. The school didn't give me any teaching materials to work with, so I made the curriculum up as we went along.

Eventually, a foreigner gave me a fax number to order English resources. It seemed like an answer to prayer, but when starting to place the order, I felt a check in my spirit. After some struggle with this, I chose not to order the books.

The next day, I met someone who was leaving for the States. She gave me a bag of books saying, "Maybe you can use these."

English resources! God had me covered.

In pursuit of more Christian fellowship, Jennifer and I took a trip to a small town called Yuxi. Some friends of hers taught at the college there.

Peter and Lauren Snyder had served in Haiti many years before coming to China. As we arrived at their old Chinese apartment, Lauren warmly greeted us as Pete chatted with another missionary on the sofa. Then he looked up, raised his hand, and burst into a high pitched shout:

"HEYYY!"

I thought, *is this guy a nut?*

After a little small talk, I tested the water for spiritual conversation. "I'm reading a book called, *Joy Unspeakable.* It's about the baptism of the Holy Spirit being the key to revival. Where are you guys on that?"

I was expecting blank stares from Pete and his guest. Instead, they jumped right in. The three of us had a great time of fellowship. Pete especially encouraged us, being no stranger to the works of the Holy Spirit.

That day marked the start of one of the most impacting friendships of my life. Pete, ten years older, gave me helpful advice for teaching English in China and valuable counsel concerning marriage. Just what I needed at the time. We hit it off that day, not realizing all the Lord would do with us together in the future.

The high school job finished the following June. By grace, I survived that incredibly challenging situation—one of the most impossible teaching environments. I shared the gospel whenever I had the chance but only got polite responses and quick conversation changes.

The classes never went very well. I failed to tap into the secret for great teaching in that difficult environment. In fact, toward the end of the term, I was just trying to bide the time, coming up with busy work for the students. It didn't seem like a good Christian witness.

At the end, however, many students asked for my address and told me they'd never forget me. Then a leader told me how all the teachers and the principal really appreciated my work.

"Me?" I said, "Why?"

"Because," she said, "you have kept up with your many classes, and you rarely missed any. Last year, the foreign teacher constantly missed her classes. Our superior got very upset with her. But we have seen how committed you are."

I told her it was because of Jesus. It was amazing how the Lord had blessed them when all the while I felt like I was failing them!

That probably happens a lot. The Lord is taking care of us and using us often in ways we are unaware of.

Isn't it good to know that God's got you covered?

English students leave shoes at the door and come in to learn songs about the Lord at Christmas time.

Pete Snyder and school officials

Chapter 13

The Teacher

"How do you get spiritually fed over there in China?"

We used to hear this often. One could easily feel isolated on the mission field. Cell phones and internet had not yet come on the scene. There was no international church. Nevertheless, a group of us met for home church each week. We sang, prayed, and took turns bringing the message. Most of us were missionaries, but sometimes others participated. Once, a businessman was scheduled to speak, but he decided to play a cassette tape instead.

"I thought we'd all get to listen to a REAL preacher today," he said.

Well, even if we weren't *real preachers,* our fellowship was good. But fellowship with Pete Snyder was special. When we got together, the Holy Spirit often entered in powerfully. As we traveled throughout the years, we stayed in dumpy hotel rooms that would become like the Ritz because God was there. Many nights were spent talking about the things of the Lord.

We continuously swapped books. Pete would call up from Yuxi and say, "I finished that one. What else you got?" We'd get excited about what the Lord was teaching us and would hardly talk about anything else when we got together.

I felt like I was getting spiritually fed better than I ever did in America. It wasn't just that we were reading edifying books, we were fellowshipping with God through them. That's what makes the difference. Whenever the Teacher is present, we get fed.

On the other hand, Christians can sit under lots of teaching, but if the life of God isn't in it, they'll remain undernourished. That's why it's important to learn from others who have the witness of God in *their lives,* and not just in their degrees, credentials, or celebrity status.

In the fall of 1996, I graduated from teaching Chinese high schoolers to teaching at the biggest university in Kunming. There I was, hardly feeling qualified, hired as a "foreign expert" because of my masters degree. During this time we made weekly trips to the local orphanage. We saw children come alive because of the love the missionaries brought week after week. Some of the Chinese workers were

Christians, and the orphanage became better because God was there working through His people. It still wasn't a wonderful place, but the missionaries and Christian workers made a huge difference.

Tragically, foreigners were eventually barred from much orphanage work in China. One foreigner had taken incriminating photos of terrible orphanage conditions in another province. Those photos were sent to western media outlets, and the story got out about how bad it was in China. That's how the devil works. He's quick to expose and bring accusation of sin. After that, the Chinese government in many cities said, "No more foreign help."

God, on the other hand, doesn't deny the ugliness inside, but He enters into it and cleans it up. He doesn't condemn, but leads us into the better way. That's what we saw working at the orphanage before the doors were shut. And that's how He works in cleaning up our lives.

Besides orphanage work, I met regularly with two Chinese men. One just wanted to practice his English, so he agreed to read the Bible with me. He became a believer. The other was a believer but needed encouraging. He grew stronger.

There were many opportunities to share the gospel with our neighbors. Since China didn't allow formal missionary activity, ministry largely consisted of simply being light and showing love. The Chinese culture didn't normally express love. It was rare for a husband or wife to even say, "I love you." There were no outward displays of affection, not even hugs at the airport after a time of separation. When we spoke kindly to a cashier, it probably gave her something to talk about for days.

This has changed, however, over time. Western media has been an influence, and the presence of God through His people has been largely instrumental.

The gospel was shared in the college classrooms. I wasn't allowed to preach, but I was free to talk about faith if students asked questions relating to it. It was also acceptable to talk about Christ if it applied to cultural studies. Christmas and Easter were ideal times to bring Him in. I managed to get creative and bring Him in often.

I became something of a pastor to four young Christians. Other students often asked me questions, and some came over to watch the video about Jesus.

Before a furlough, one girl asked, "When you leave, who can I talk to about these things?" I arranged for her to meet a Chinese sister, who later led her to salvation.

That's how it often worked. The Lord used a number of witnesses to reach out to the students. It didn't matter who actually led them in a prayer of commitment. It was just good to be a part of the process. "I planted," said Paul, "Apollos watered, but God gave the increase" (1Corinthians 3:6).

It was back to America that summer. Jennifer was expecting, and I got a job teaching Public Speaking at the University of Cincinnati. We stayed until our son Matthew was born.

I felt like I had more freedom to share the gospel in the Chinese classrooms than I did in America! However, I did have moments. One girl stood up to give a speech on the religion, Scientology. She started by asking the class, "Have you ever wondered about the meaning of life?"

She proceeded with a dull presentation, and later told me it seemed better when she rehearsed it. Maybe the Holy Spirit intervened!

But at the end of class, I know He intervened.

I shared that *I knew the meaning of life,* and if anyone was interested they could catch me after class. Instead, they practically begged me to tell them right then and there. God moved in that room. A student caught up with me later and described it as "fire." He wanted to know more.

I met with him and gave him some reading material, but I fear I may have come on too strong. I still needed to learn to be sensitive and let God do the teaching.

Meanwhile Jennifer and I became friends with a Chinese family that ran a restaurant in our neighborhood. They wanted us to teach their son English, and they fed us in return. It's been years, and their son has moved on. But the restaurant is still there. To this day they insist on giving us free food, but we still try to pay.

Our son Matthew was born, and four months later we moved back to China where we were about to become pioneers.

Once again, we had a lot of luggage full of goods we couldn't buy overseas. Diapers are heavier than you think!

Chapter 14

Unless the Lord Builds the House

It's not always adventuresome on the mission field. Kunming greeted us with dashed expectations. We had hoped to move to a more remote region, but the doors didn't open. The doors didn't even open for teaching college again in Kunming. Instead, the International School invited us with "we'll find something for you to do" in mind.

We wanted to go where there were no other foreigners. One city looked good, about seven hours away towards Vietnam, but there was no college there. That meant no legal way for us to live there. However, a nearby city, Mengzi, had a school. We just didn't know anybody who could connect us.

A placement agency located in Hong Kong might have been able to help. They sent all kinds of forms to fill out, along with a hefty fee. But after praying about it, Jennifer and I decided not to go through a tedious application process just to make a possible connection with the school. It was tempting to try to make things happen, but we decided to wait and see what God might do.

Instead of teaching Chinese college students in a remote region, I ended up tutoring children in ESL (English as a Second Language) at the International School in Kunming. It was a disappointing time.

But disappointments can lead to divine appointments. At Thanksgiving, I visited the Chinese campus where I used to teach, hoping to run into some of my old students outside.

Everyone was still in class. *Came at the wrong time,* I thought.

I locked my bike and went into the English building. Passing my old classroom, I peeked through the door window expecting to see a different group of students.

Instead, all my students were there, just like before! They saw me and got excited. Their teacher, a Chinese woman, turned around to see what was happening. I left quickly, thinking she'd yelled at me for disrupting her class. But instead she chased me in the hall to say, "Come back! They want to see you!"

It was a happy reunion. Before long, one of the students raised her hand and asked, "Can we sing the Christmas songs you taught us?" Teaching Christmas songs about Jesus was one of the ways I shared the gospel with them. It was wonderful to see that they still held these songs in their hearts.

The teacher, Mrs. Xi, turned out to be a Christian. She invited me to bring Jennifer, Matthew, and my guitar to a special class for a Christmas party.

We went and played the songs. Unbeknownst to us, a student recorded them. He later had his friend play them on a local radio station. Although it was in English, Jesus was praised on the Chinese airwaves!

A friendship developed with Mrs. Xi, who happened to be from Mengzi, the city we wanted to teach in.

"I'm going home to Mengzi in two weeks," she said.

"See if you can get us a job at the college," I joked.

She replied that she had friends there and would ask about it if she had a chance. Life went on, and I thought nothing more about it.

But two weeks later, Mrs. Xi called. "They're looking for a teacher!" she reported. She gave me the school president's phone number. Ordinarily one would have to go through the Foreign Affairs department. This was going straight to the top. Mustering up the nerve, I called him and set up a time to visit the college.

I asked Pete Snyder to come along. He was setting up sister school relationships with Chinese colleges and schools in the States. He didn't think he could do that in Mengzi, but he went with me to pray.

It turned out, however, that the president was very interested in working with Pete. The two of them became fast friends. It felt like I was just tagging along. But it ended well, with the president eager to have me move down and teach.

The school was located outside of the city, which itself was quite remote. Jennifer said, "Take some pictures while you're there." But there wasn't much to the place. Clouds settled upon it so I couldn't take any good shots. I wondered how we would do living at the school, being so cut off from the conveniences we knew in Kunming. Mengzi was poor and underdeveloped. It was going to be a challenge, but I felt assured it was God's will.

It was a little troubling when the president took me aside and said, "As you know, China is still a communist nation. So you must not try to spread your religion or give out literature of that sort."

This would be a tight situation. Here we would live on a small campus and be closely watched. It didn't take long to be given the prohibition against spreading religion, and we hadn't even moved there yet.

"Now we know that God is going to work in Mengzi," said Pete. "That president has made it impossible to do something, and that's just the kind of situation God moves in!"

How could it not happen? The Lord was already working. We initially didn't know how to connect with the school, but He made a way. And He made it easy.

God gave me a dream. There was a long moving wall with an opening farther in the distance. The opening was getting closer, but instead of waiting for it, I tried to climb the wall in order to get to the other side. Trying to climb the moving wall was bumbling and stressful. It would have been easier to just wait for the opening to come along.

The Lord had made an opening for us in Mengzi. In the same way, we could trust Him to make openings for the gospel to change lives in that area. And we don't have to stress out about future opportunities. It's good to knock on doors, but there's no need to force them. "Unless the LORD builds the house, they labor in vain who build it" (Psalm 127:1).

The school scheduled us to start that fall. It was exciting to think about being the representatives of Christ in an area that was mostly barren and unreached.

Pete and I stayed the night in a dumpy guest house on the campus. As the mosquitos swarmed around the dangling light bulb from the ceiling, we knelt by our hard beds and had a powerful time of prayer. We knew we were invading the devil's territory and making way for a new work of God. We claimed the area as taken for the glory of Jesus.

Seven years later, Mengzi saw all kinds of renewal and revival. The city literally transformed when the local government decided to move their offices there. It became one of the best places to visit in the province. The college expanded into a University and the campus blossomed with new buildings and renovations. Other missionaries came. Both teachers and students put their faith in Jesus. We believed God blessed it all because of the increasing presence of His people there.

But Pete and I could hardly wait to get out of there from that first trip. It was the eve of the Chinese New Year, so taxis to Kunming were rare. After fruitlessly trying to get a taxi, we resolved to wait for the one bus to Kunming. But it came late and was stuffed full. It would be a very difficult six hour ride. As we were about to board it, a driver approached from out of nowhere.

"You guys want to hire a taxi instead?" It was as if an angel appeared.

We saw that taxi as a special gift, and another sign that God was starting to build His house for us in Mengzi. It was exciting to think about the possibilities ahead.

But there was still a period of waiting to get through. In the meantime, something special was about to happen in Kunming.

Hmong People

Campus in Mengzi

Chapter 15

Hurry Up and Wait!

With months to go before moving to Mengzi, it was hard to be patient. The devil kept telling me, "It won't go through. You'll lose that job just like before." I remembered how the school in Kunming withdrew their offer. But one night in a prayer meeting, someone spoke Revelation 3:8 as a special word to me: "I know your works. See, I have set before you an open door, and no man can shut it." I grabbed that and held on to it, recalling it whenever the devil brought up the matter.

A.B. Simpson's book, *In the School of Faith,* encouraged me. It talked about times of waiting and how God prepares us in such times. The Lord has a plan and a due season, just as He had for Moses. When Moses tried to take action before God's time, it had negative results (see Exodus 2:11-14).

Though I wanted to move right away, I knew the work wouldn't be blessed going ahead of God.

In our culture, we want everything done yesterday! But the Lord looks at time differently. He's patient with us when we give Him no reason to be. Yet we often become impatient with God when there's every reason to trust Him. He knows best.

He has reasons for the delays. Often it's because we're not ready for the blessing or assignment yet. It would be too much for us to handle. Or in some cases, God's got more to bless us with in our current situation. There are still things He wants to accomplish before taking us to the next phase.

If we hadn't stayed in Kunming during that season, Jennifer and I would have missed one of the happiest days of our lives.

Two children at the orphanage had won our hearts. Little Guang, whom we called Jessica, was a sweet and spunky little girl. At one time she was close to getting adopted, but something went wrong. I remember holding her on my lap and weeping over her. She was encouraged to keep praying for a family.

Then there was little Pan, or Jonathan. He came to the orphanage in bad shape. He nearly died of malnutrition and dehydration until the Christian workers rescued him. He literally came back to life under their care and became a healthy child. As usual, it was the result of God's presence and love that made the difference.

Jennifer and I got to be with both of these children when they met their new parents on the same day.

Our Dutch friend Robbie worked regularly at the orphanage. He had prepped Jessica.

"Jessica," he said, "do you know what an airplane is?"

"A big machine that flies in the sky!"

"Yes," he said. Then he showed her a picture of the Nichols' family. "Do you know whose family this is?"

"No," she said.

"This is YOUR new family, and they're coming soon."

Jessica's eyes widened. Then Robbie added, "You will be going with them on an airplane in just a few days!"

The Roberts came for Jonathan at the same time the Nichols came for Jessica. Both were Christian families and both fathers were pastors. They knew how close we were to the kids and invited us to be there when they met them. That was basically unheard of. It was the greatest honor and blessing to be there as the children met their new parents. To top it off, they all came to our apartment afterwards for a celebration cake.

Years later, Jennifer and I talked to a teenaged Jessica in English on the phone in America! We even became Facebook friends. We also visited Jonathan with the Roberts family in New York.

We saw those kids go through many trials, and we saw them brought into loving families. We would not have wanted to miss that day in Kunming when they all came together. It was a tremendous blessing in the wilderness of waiting.

It was good that we weren't yet living on the college campus in Mengzi. Campuses got agitated after May 8, 1999 when NATO forces bombed a Chinese embassy in Yugoslavia. The conflict there had been intense already, and the bombing of the embassy (said to be a mistake) caused great outrage in China. Two journalists were killed. The Chinese media stirred up the people's anger with continual anti-American sentiments and propaganda. Students were encouraged to protest, and the streets streamed with demonstrations. Violence erupted in several places. For the first time we felt unwelcome in China.

Chinese friends called to check on us. "We are still your friends," they reassured us. "Don't go near any parks or college campuses. It's better if you stay inside for a while."

I still had to go to work at the International School. That week I rode my bicycle each day amid icy stares.

One day I went to lunch with a British friend. The server asked us the usual question, "Where are you from?"

"England," my friend said. I just kept my mouth shut.

It was scary to see how quickly the nation could be influenced the way they were at that time. And then, after about a week of tension and anger, the government told everyone to get on with their lives and to "turn your anger into determination to build up a better China."

After that, I stopped to get my bike fixed. The Chinese repairman, an older man wearing a traditional communist cap, asked, "Where are you from?"

I said sheepishly, "America," expecting the politeness to turn to ice. Instead, the man grinned from ear to ear and gave me a big thumbs up.

"You Americans are GREAT!" he beamed.

The older population loved America because they remembered our help before and during World War II.

It was good to get a smile again. Everything went back to normal. We just had to wait it out. God knows the times and seasons. There are reasons for delays. Hebrews 6:12 says not to "become sluggish, but imitate those who through faith and PATIENCE inherit the promises."

Chapter 16

Burdens and Breakthroughs

The move to Mengzi didn't go smoothly. Much of our furniture got beaten up on the way down. After arriving, we climbed five floors to an apartment that wasn't ready. We opened the door and found it cluttered with boxes and furniture that wasn't ours. There was hardly any room to bring anything in. So we waited while the school found a place to move and store everything.

They sent students to help. There was no elevator, so the stairwell bustled with traffic as their furniture came down and ours went up.

Hours later, as it began to get dark, we discovered there were no lights in the place. Each room had a bare socket hanging from the ceiling, but somebody had forgotten to put in the bulbs!

The campus was surrounded by small villages and beautiful mountains. It seemed we had gone back in time. Kunming wasn't very developed but seemed progressive compared to here.

I was the only foreign teacher, but three other American couples came at that time to study Chinese. This was a result of Pete's working with the school president to start a language program for foreigners.

It was as if God had popped a hole in this region, and now His people were moving in. Certainly the devil was not going to sit back without a fight. Thousands of years of bondage to the local principalities and powers weren't going to give way so easily. At times I sensed a dark presence in the area and felt heavy spiritual burdens. Prayer was essential.

It was almost all that could be done. People didn't want to talk about the Lord. Every time I tried to bring Him up in conversation, they would quickly change the topic.

"Have you ever heard about Jesus?"

"No."

"Jesus came that we might know God."

"Really? Oh, I like your shoes. Did you get them in China?"

Not only was the ground spiritually frozen, but the leaders of the school had warned teachers and students not to get too close to the foreigners or talk about religion.

Other than those assigned to us by the Foreign Affairs office, only two retired teachers initially befriended us. These two elderly men had served 20 years in a labor camp during the Chinese Cultural Revolution. Their crime: they were English teachers. English was considered counter revolutionary during that historical nightmare.

Mr. Gao and Mr. Bao knew each other in the camp, but they weren't permitted to speak to each other the entire time there. When we met them, they were both living on campus and enjoying retired life. And though we thought the living conditions were poor, they never had it so good.

Mr. Gao was always happy to talk about God but seemed he would never commit his life to Jesus. He just enjoyed the intellectual conversation. But several Christians interacted with him and never gave up. He was a friend to all, and a couple of years before he died, he became our brother in the Lord.

It took time for the spiritually frozen ground to thaw. The first two years were discouraging. No one seemed to care about hearing the gospel. But just before I left for the summer, two students came over to practice English.

I said something about the Lord to them and expected the topic to change as usual. To my surprise, one of them, Steven, asked questions and expressed interest. It was a breakthrough! The other student tried to change the topic, but Steven quickly brought it back again and asked more questions about God. We actually talked about the Lord for more than an hour, and then I gave him a Bible.

"Read this while I'm gone, and if you have any questions ask one of the other foreigners here."

He agreed, and I left for the States encouraged. Something had finally broke in the spiritual realm.

Steven graduated, so I didn't see him again when I returned. But I heard that he had prayed with one of the foreigners to receive Christ.

After that, he met a group of Chinese Christians from Hong Kong who helped him understand more. Then he started working with some Baptist missionaries in Kunming. And in 2008 I ran into him. He had started running his own business as a means to fund mission projects throughout the province and beyond. He invited me to work with him on an outreach project in Myanmar. I jumped at the opportunity, and since then we have been on many adventures together.

Steven is one of the greatest missionaries I have ever known. I have pleaded with him to write his own book about his experiences, but I don't know that he will. I take great joy, though, when he introduces me to his friends as, "This is Rick. He was my English teacher. He was the first one to tell me about Jesus and give me a Bible."

We returned to the States in the summer of 2001. Jennifer was expecting. On September 11, Matthew, only three years old, was playing around with the clock radio where we were staying. He kept turning it on and off. When we heard talk about planes crashing into buildings, we stopped him.

"Keep this on!!"

We listened in shock for a while, but it didn't really hit home until we saw the images on television.

At that time I had been caught up in different email debates and conversations concerning theological issues. I had been digging through Scriptures to prove my points, but had neglected reading the Word simply out of love for God. Thus I found my heart failing for fear during the continuous reports of terrorism.

Anthrax was being sent through the mail. Watching the news each night fed into fear and made me wonder what kind of world our children were going to grow up in.

I knew as a Christian I shouldn't be a bundle of nerves, but I was. Finally, the Lord reminded me of a sermon I once read by Charles Spurgeon, "Jesus Asleep on a Pillow." It was about how to sleep in a storm, and how we could have peace because Jesus was in our boat. It brought comfort. That and other devotional reading got grace working in my heart again, and I had a breakthrough of peace. Fear was destroyed by meditating on psalms like Psalms 27, 46, 91, 112, and 121.

"The Word of God is living and powerful, and sharper than any two-edged sword" (Hebrews 4:12), but we have to use the sword properly. The Word of God changes us when we read it for the purpose to be changed. Otherwise, we may learn a lot ABOUT the sword, and even win some theological debates, but still be unable to use it victoriously in our lives.

Our son Ryan was born in October. In March we entered the new world of post 9-11 airport security to fly back to China. It's good to prevent terrorism. But it seemed ridiculous when they pulled us aside, a young couple with two small children, to do a random check of our large amount of luggage.

After six years, we finished up our time in Mengzi. Some of our favorite people at the school became Christians. Other missionaries kept the fire going. Seven years after we first came, they reported revival among the students.

We moved back to Kunming because the Lord was leading me to travel more with Pete Snyder. He was working with school building projects in the countryside. We traveled to rural villages and also took groups who had helped fund the new schools. The Chinese government matched the funds. Because of these schools, we could get into many unreached areas and have a valid reason for being there. The government officials themselves went with us and became good friends. Some of them eventually became Christians.

We saw great changes in the Chinese officials even if they didn't become Christians. When we first started working with them, they would dress sloppily, take us to dumpy restaurants, and get sloshing drunk. Over the years we rubbed off on them. They started looking nicer, took us to better places, and before eating they'd ask, "Would you like to pray first?" The drinking also lightened up. The presence of God's people makes a difference in the atmosphere.

What a privilege it is to be His representatives, wherever we go. "For we are His workmanship, created in Christ Jesus for good works, which God prepared beforehand that we should walk in them" (Ephesians 2:10). The good works aren't ours but HIS. We just walk in them. That takes the burden off of us and gives Him the opportunity to bring the breakthroughs.

Praise God!

Old school classroom,
new school classroom

Chapter 17

A Spy and a Pseudonym

As travels to the countryside increased, our finances decreased. It didn't help that the cost of living in Kunming went up. As a result, we left for the States in the summer of 2004 without enough money for a return ticket. Even so, we planned to return in the fall and move back to Mengzi.

We weren't flat broke, but it was unclear how everything was going to come together. On top of this, I believed we were supposed to buy a jeep. So prayers went up for the jeep when it seemed crazy to even think about it.

God was faithful. Not only did we make it back, but a month later we had the money to buy the jeep.

And the Lord gave us a new road to go with it! A highway opened up between Kunming and Mengzi, cutting off about two hours of travel time. We took it often.

I continued to travel to the countryside and often met up with Pete. At other times I connected with groups who wanted to help with the schools and took them into the mountain areas.

There were many opportunities to witness for Jesus. We gave Bibles to teachers and even government officials. We brought shoes and jackets to the kids in the schools and told them about God's love. We shared the gospel at school opening ceremonies. There was a measure of freedom in what could be done as long as it didn't cross certain lines with the Chinese government.

One of those lines was making public invitations to pray and receive Christ. Groups that came with us were told not to do this. They could speak at the opening ceremonies of the schools they helped fund. They could share that Jesus died for them and rose again. But they were not to turn it into an evangelistic meeting. Up until 2005 there was never a problem, as everyone complied with this restriction.

Then one group came and ruined everything.

"I know you said not to do that," they told Pete, "but we just felt that's what God wanted us to do!"

They didn't know it, but there was a spy present when they asked the children publicly to raise their hands to receive Christ. The spy alerted the authorities, who in turn took the group in for questioning.

That local government basically closed the door on future involvement with us. They also punished the officials who had traveled with us for years, our good friends. They were demoted and given undesirable jobs.

But the group got to go back to America and write compelling newsletters about being persecuted in China.

The government eventually permitted us to return and bring supplies to the schools, but we had to work with new officials. They were only interested in our money. They wouldn't let us be open with the gospel, and they confiscated our Chinese Bibles.

Nonetheless, God would not be thwarted. Years later, Pete met some Chinese pastors and introduced them to these areas. They started sending their own local missionaries down. They would not be watched like us foreigners, and they could preach the gospel to their own people. Over time, the seeds that were planted produced a harvest. Today there are churches in several of those areas because of the schools and all who helped fund them.

In each of these areas we interacted with different Chinese ethnic groups, including Yi, Zhuang, and Hmong people. Many of these people only spoke their own ethnic language, so we had to depend on someone to translate our Chinese for them. And often we needed help with our

Chinese! But we managed to get the message through to some degree.

In 2006, some Hmong Christians from Thailand came to Mengzi. I took them to the Hmong areas we previously worked in. It was exciting to see them share the gospel in their own tongue and know that it was being communicated effectively. It was exciting to give Hmong Bibles to the people. One farmer said he was the only one in the village who could read, but that he would read it out loud to everybody.

I had wondered in the past how we could ever reach these villages, since we couldn't speak their language. The best we could do was pray and show them love. But God knew that years later I could take some of their own people from Thailand to get the job done! I would have never guessed it. If you wonder how God is going to work in your situation, just remember that God can still work wonders.

We went back to the States in July 2006, and I was asked to give a morning devotion at American Family Radio, a ministry based in Tupelo. After the devotion, one of the radio newsmen asked me if I would do a brief interview. They would edit most of it and then broadcast only a snippet on the air. That sounded safe enough. A short snippet shouldn't cause any problems. And what would be the chances of any Chinese government officials tuning in to an American Christian radio station at just the right time?

A week or two later, a friend from Cincinnati sent an email saying, "Hey Rick! Saw this this morning. Is it safe to have this information out there?" Below his text, he forwarded a screenshot from a big Christian website called Crosswalk.com:

Religion Today Summaries - July 24, 2006
Compiled & Edited by Crosswalk Editorial Staff

Daily briefs of the top news stories impacting Christians around the world.

Missionary to China Suggests Different Approach with Chinese Govt.

An evangelical missionary who spent more than ten years in China says while he can't tell the communist government there everything he is doing, he hasn't had to be completely secretive either, reports *AgapePress*. Rick Bell and his family are back in the United States on furlough but intend to return to the Hunan province of China in February. Bell says some missionaries get into trouble with the authorities because they are too secretive. "You can't say, 'Hey, I'm a missionary.' You have to be there doing something legitimate in their eyes," he explains. "However, you don't have to be secretive all the time. There are some missionaries who go there, and they won't tell anything to anybody about why they're there, which we believe is not the proper approach." Bell, who is with Global Outreach International, explains the approach he uses. "In our case, we develop relationships with the officials, and through the proper channels, in legitimate ways, we're free to share with them relationally about why we're there," the missionary says. "We're there because we love the Lord, and we want to share God's love with the Chinese- and they accept that." Bell and his family have served in China since 1995.

What a shock! Not only was my name out there, but also our sending organization, Global Outreach. That could get us in trouble.

At the same time it was amusing. What a funny thing to wake up and find out you're famous! They didn't tell me they were going to syndicate the interview and distribute the report to several different Christian news outlets. But it didn't bother me. I figured that God had us covered, and that it ultimately wouldn't be a security issue.

However, when I related this incident to the director at Global Outreach, he didn't think it was funny. He ran over to American Family Radio and insisted they fix it.

They did. Subsequent radio reports and news clippings around the web referred to me as "Wayne Raymond," and the name of Global Outreach was dropped.

Chapter 18

Grace in the Trial

Five year old Ryan came up to Jennifer and out of the blue said, "Mommy, I think you have a baby sister in your pouch." Jennifer responded with a little science lesson on marsupials, and clarified that she had no pouch, but took it in stride. Later when we found out she really was expecting, and that the baby was indeed a girl, we thought we should listen when Ryan told us, "Her name is Mary."

Before Marybeth's arrival, doctors discovered that she had a single ventricle heart defect and would need a series of surgeries (known as the Fontan Pathway) to save her life. That news was hard to take, but we were thankful that we had some time to prepare for it. Sometimes the condition isn't detected until the baby is born.

We hoped for a miracle and a good report with each new visit to the doctor. But simply hoping and praying for a ys good enough. We didn't know how to

...iises in Scripture and pray in faith for

...

There are many Scriptures that promise healing to those who would dare believe them (see for example, Ex.15:6; Is. 53:4-6; Matt.8:17; Ps.103:3-4; Prov.4:22). But often Christians chalk their sicknesses up to God's 'mysterious' will or to some form of discipline. Jesus never placed sickness on anybody. Instead, He told us that it is *the thief* that comes "to steal, and to kill, and to destroy." (John 10:10).

There are many in the church who won't resist that thief, because they think it's God that's stricken them. Or, they only believe that God *can heal* but not sure *that He's willing.*

But the Word gives ample evidence that He is willing (Mark 1:41; 3John 2), that God cares for our bodies (1Cor.6:13; 1Thess.5:23), and that He's already secured healing for us (Is.53:5, 1Pet.2:24). When I started to understand this, I saw more healings take place.

Nonetheless, God still blessed us at the time. We enjoyed living like a normal American family in Cincinnati. When the situation seemed darker than brighter, the Lord gave strength. He led me to consider how things got worse for Joseph before his eventual exaltation. Things got worse for

Moses and the children of Israel before they were delivered from Egypt. Things got worse for David before he was granted his promised throne. And the worst came at the cross at Calvary, before Jesus rose from the dead so that eternal life could be offered to all. Praise God that HE is our hope, and He is not intimidated by our circumstances!

Contrary to traditional Christian teaching, the trials in life do not in themselves strengthen or help us to grow. If they did, almost everyone would be a strong and mature Christian. It's the Word that strengthens and helps us to grow. Trials are simply opportunities to exercise faith in the Word. Scripture doesn't teach us to embrace trials, but to be joyful in spite of them. That's possible because faith can work in the midst of them.

We believed for a miracle. Although the miracle didn't come the way we wanted it, God still came through, and we had our bounciest baby yet! Below is an excerpt from our newsletter at that time:

Global Outreach International

P.O. Box 1 Tupelo MS 38802

Chi... ppenings with the Bells 为中国祷告

Rick, Jennifer, Matthew, Ryan , & Marybeth

Baby progress report. Since Marybeth was born in March and had her first heart surgery on March 30, she has done better than we could have ever hoped. <u>Thank you so much for praying for her.</u>

- We did not have to keep her on a feeding tube but for a few days, and the doctors said that it might be a few weeks!
- We were told she might have trouble gaining weight, but she has put on the pounds without any problem!
- We were told to watch for excessive sweating when nursing, or shortness of breath, but all has been well.
- We were told that because of her heart defect, her lips, hands and feet might turn purple during this time, but so far that has not happened.

The day of her first surgery, the Lord comforted me with His Word from **Psalm 46:5: God is in the midst of her; she shall not be moved: God shall help her, and that right early.**

This word, I believe, refers generally to the people of God. But that day it was as if it was speaking directly about our baby. Now four months later we gratefully declare its fulfillment. We did not get a miraculous healing as we would have liked, but it has been as if everything is normal- you could not tell she has any problem, except that we have to give her medicine twice a day. Jesus is **gracious, and full of compassion, and righteous (Ps.112:4).** He has made light arise in the darkness.

Marybeth had her second surgery four months later and all went well. In November we packed up, left our rented Cincinnati home and flew back to China. This time, a spiritual revolution awaited us.

Chapter 19

A Change in the Atmosphere

Now a family of five, we returned to Kunming late on a rainy night and stayed in a friend's empty apartment. For the first time in 12 years of living in China, culture shock set in.

Why this time?

Perhaps it was because we had lived like a normal family in America for almost a year. We had rented a nice house, drove two cars, got involved in church and the community, and I worked as an adjunct instructor. There were no cultural differences to deal with. Everyone understood our language. And anything we needed could be ordered online and brought straight to our door!

All of that changed, and more change was in the air.

Instead of working for a school, the Lord led me to start an English consulting company. This would free me up to travel more and would provide a visa while visas were getting harder to obtain.

Our family got visas just before new regulations restricted foreign companies and made them costlier to start. Then when summer came, Beijing hosted the 2008 Olympics and temporarily shut the door on any new foreign company startups.

God brought it all together at just the right time.

We found the apartment we would live in until the end of our stay in China. Apartments came unfinished, and it was up to the renters to fix them up. We hired workers to paint, put in flooring, build cabinets, redo bathrooms, and install light fixtures. It took them a month before we could move in, and it drained most of our finances. The U.S. dollar was steadfastly losing value, and prices in China were steadily increasing. Yet we had all that we needed.

Once settled, Pete gave me a CD that someone had mailed him. "Here, listen to this," he said. "You won't believe what a difference it will make!"

"Oh right," I replied, "Everybody says that. I've been given so many tapes and CDs." To be honest, I was weary with a lot of preaching.

"Yeah, but this one is DIFFERENT. If this guy is right, we've been wrong about a lot of things."

That sounded dramatic, but it didn't convince me. "Well what does he talk about?"

"Just listen to it!"

That ended the discussion, and I, the skeptic, took the CD home.

I planned to give it ten minutes. Then I could truthfully say I heard it, if asked.

The message's title was, "The War is Over," by a guy named Andrew Wommack. Ten minutes went quickly, and I didn't want to turn it off. Before I knew it, an hour and fifteen minutes had passed and I was hungry for more.

Who is this guy? I thought. When I found his website, I discovered that "The War is Over" was a series. There were four other messages to it. I forwarded the link to Pete, and we started devouring everything that Andrew had online.

What made the difference? For the first time it became clear to me that grace is more than just tolerance, or what gets us to heaven. The love of God is more than just a "tolerant" love that accepts us in the end. His grace makes us acceptable *now*. Because of grace, He's happy with me now, in spite of my falling so short of the standard.

Many Christians seem to understand the forgiveness of God, but not so much *the acceptance of God*. They still look to their works in order to please God. They still struggle daily with trying to become righteous, and then grieve when they fail. That's not trusting in Jesus. God "made Him who knew no sin to be sin for us, that we might become the righteousness of God in Him" (2Cor.5:21). Trusting in Jesus means believing we are already made righteous.

Like salvation, righteousness is a gift (Rom.5:17). It's because of the exchange that was made at the cross. We can't add to that or take away from it.

That's grace! No more worrying about trying to measure up. Jesus measured up for us, and we are "accepted in the Beloved" (Eph.1:6). We can rejoice in God instead of grieve over shortcomings and failures.

Grace doesn't give a license to sin, but it brings power to change. It's knowing the goodness of God that leads to repentance (Rom.2:4). When love affects the heart, godliness results.

On the other hand, fearing God's anger and displeasure may bring some temporary outward change, but the heart remains unmoved. When inevitable failure comes, there's grief and stress over "how hard it is to live for Jesus." Tradition reinforces this and teaches us to think of ourselves as strugglers to the end, as opposed to being new creations in Christ (2Cor.5:17).

You say, "But Rick, you knew about grace and love. It got you to China!"

Yes, I knew it. But it was always being pushed to the back by teachings that subtly promoted a works mentality.

Andrew Wommack came in and tore down many traditional barriers that kept me from enjoying God's grace and walking in its power. I didn't know it, but I was a legalist. Pete was the same, and we were both radically changed, along with our wives.

I became less judgmental of others because I quit judging myself. If God had grace and wasn't angry with me, why should I be angry with others? My marriage even got better.

When we came back to America, someone asked Jennifer, "What happened to Rick? He's sure lightened up!" I distributed my first book, *Win Christ,* everywhere we went. It was an attempt to more fully teach what I've just shared here. It was well received and has since blessed many. And Pete and I have seen this message bring revival to the Chinese church.

For years I taught English classes and had limited contact with the Chinese church. I remember coming back from classes frustrated. "Lord, I just taught them Peter Piper Picked a Peck of Pickled Peppers," I prayed. "When can I teach the Bible?" And for years there was no answer.

Looking back, I'm glad there wasn't. The Chinese church did NOT need fire and brimstone preaching. They did NOT need the guilt producing sermons I was likely to give. The Chinese church was already decidedly legalistic. The culture itself was very duty oriented.

Doors remained shut until the Lord got grace into me.

After this happened, I reconnected with my former student Steven. We took off and started working together on projects in Burma and near Laos. Around that same time, the Lord opened the door for Pete to work with one of the largest house church networks in China. He brought me along, and it was all about teaching the WORD. No more silly tongue twisters!

The day had come. Our ministry took on a new direction. We no longer worked with school leaders and government officials in an effort to shine the light. We now partnered with the growing house church movement in China to fulfill the Great Commission (Matt. 28:19-20). This partnership increased the extent and reach of the light. It was like going from flickering a small flame to igniting a wildfire.

Chapter 20

How Are We Going to Get Out of Here?

Dangerous roads were nothing new. Most of the previous school building projects were in hard to get to areas. It was fun to watch visitors' reactions as we careened curves on narrow dirt roads with dangerous drop-offs high up in the mountains.

Coming down from such places would even be scarier, and you'd hope the brakes would keep working and the mud sliding would be minimal. Once safe on level ground, there would still be hours of relentless bouncing up and down on rocks and dirt.

There was nothing like getting onto a main road after that. The transition from the rocky bouncing to smooth riding brought a happy sense of peace and calm. Maybe that's an example of how it will be when we transition from this troubling world into the righteous kingdom of God.

I never thought much about the danger on those roads until I started travelling with my former English student, Steven. We met up again in 2008 and started traveling to countryside villages in some of the hardest to get to places.

"Do you want to help us get into Burma?" Steven asked as we ate Chinese noodles.

"YES!" I blurted out enthusiastically. But inside I heard myself thinking, *are you crazy? That sounds dangerous!*

"We can go there and we can also go to some places near the border of Laos. Those are still in China, but the Burma project is in Burma." Steven had managed to raise money for some cheap land in a special economic zone. He planned to start a farm project in a village to reach the people there with the gospel. He would send members of his church to spend three months at a time to live and work the farm. Then he would rotate other members to stay there the next three months, and so on.

The Chinese could freely get into this area, but not a foreigner like me. So I started off driving them to the border and bringing supplies. With help from the Christian Motorcycle Association, I got motorcycles for them, including a three wheeler with a flatbed for hauling supplies and farm equipment.

We made several trips, and each time the missionary farmers would come up to meet us. We took them out to eat and had times of prayer and Bible study. And each time at the border Steven asked, "Why don't you come with us and see the farm?"

"I can't," I answered. "If I were caught over there I would get in big trouble."

"Oh it's so remote," he argued, "no one is going to know you are there."

"What about the checkpoint at the border?" I asked, thinking that should settle it.

"We can go a different way. There's a way through the mountains with no checkpoint. Trust me. You will be safe. Just wear a farmer's hat or something so you look more like the people!"

We had this conversation often, but the time came when I had to seriously consider going. Steven had pressed harder than before, and I wondered if it was of the Lord.

"Father," I prayed, "is this of You? It really seems like I should go, and Steven assures me it shouldn't be a problem. I believe You have me here for a reason, and I have so much invested in this. Is it okay for me to go this one time and see it?"

A scripture came to mind. "The LORD shall preserve your going out and your coming in from this time forth and even forevermore" (Psalm 121:8). That seemed to be my green light.

"How's the road through the mountains," I asked, "and how far is it from here?" I would be driving them in the jeep.

Steven gave the standard reply, "It's not far."

I'd heard that before. That reply was given often with no variation or qualification. A journey could take half a day and still be "it's not far."

However, this time Steven did give some extra information about the road. "It's not bad, but part of it's like that road we took last time near Laos."

Oh no, I thought. *What had I gotten myself into?* That road was nothing but 4-wheelin' through the mud with various "are we going to make it" spots! On that trip, we had gone to encourage three new believers. Before we left, three more people came to faith in Jesus. Well worth it, BUT THAT ROAD!

"It's just for part of the road in," Steven said, which didn't reassure me.

I've been on scary roads before, but this won the prize. It was three hours of slippery mud, steep inclines and narrow curves around the mountains, often with complete drop offs to the side. It wasn't hard to be "praying always" (Eph.6:18) during this ride.

Once we came to the end of the mountain road we had to drive across the shallow section of a river. After that, we went up another mountain and arrived at our destination. We parked the jeep and hiked a ways to the farm.

It was magical. There was such beauty and peace at the farm site. My nerves started to recover. The joy of the Lord entered in. And if I stood still in just the right spot, my cell phone could get a signal to call Jennifer.

For two days, I became a farmer and helped them break up the ground to plant fruit trees. We also studied the Word together. It was an encouraging time.

The plan was to leave early on the third day. The night before, however, I awoke and heard nature whistling. Then it got louder, and the wind began to blow violently. The bamboo walls rattled, and I thought the roof might fly away at any second. I started to pack my clothes so that they wouldn't fly away as well.

The noise of the wind unsettled me, until I had my "wait a minute" moment. I mustered up some nerve and dared to rebuke the wind, just like Jesus.

"PEACE, BE STILL!"

And it stopped just like that!

With a "Thank you, Jesus" and a sigh of relief, I laid back down to sleep. However, it was only a few minutes later that another sound began to threaten. *This can't be good,* I thought, as sporadic drops of rain began to plip and plop upon the rooftop. *That road was bad enough,* I continued, *but if it rains, how are we going to get out of here?*

The plip plops got heavier and more frequent. Before long, it began to downpour. I thought about the possibility of being stuck in Burma. I started to wonder if I might get caught and go to jail. The devil will always give worst case scenarios to focus on in a crisis. I made the mistake of entertaining them and started to panic.

Then it dawned on me. Just like before, I sat up and commanded the rain, "In the name of Jesus, PEACE, BE STILL!"

This time it didn't work. So I tried again. But it seemed the rain was hard of hearing that night! And I sank into fear because I allowed worrisome thoughts to play through in my mind. Instead, I should have focused on the promise that was given to me, "The LORD shall preserve your going out and your coming in from this time forth and even forevermore" (Psalm 121:8).

The Lord did preserve us. The rain ended by dawn. Although it was heavy, the tropical heat dried it up enough for us to leave, though later than planned. There were still wet and slippery places on the ride back, and in some spots I had to let everyone out of the vehicle while I maneuvered it around dangerous curves at snail speed.

Maybe I shouldn't have gone in the first place. Although there was no checkpoint on the route we took, it still wasn't according to the law. We're to "obey God rather than men" (Acts 5:29) when a law would violate God's ways. Otherwise, the law should be heeded.

Nonetheless, grace prevailed. It was ultimately a blessing to be there, and we got out safe and sound.

Today that area has a thriving church. Many have trusted in the Lord and some have been healed in the neighboring villages. Steven's group even started a school for the Burmese children.

Whenever the villagers ask, "Why are you helping us?" the gospel is always shared in turn.

Burma village

Chapter 21

How Are We Going to Get Out of Here? The Sequel

In another part of the province, a minister with the local government church spoke to his leaders.

"My wife and I want to take the gospel into the mountains bordering Laos," said Minister Zhang.

"It is forbidden. You will do no such thing," the leaders replied.

Zhang and his wife didn't know what to do. God had put that area on their hearts and they must obey Him rather than men. So they quit their job with the church and spent all they had to buy some cheap farm land near the Laos border. They could live off the land but they needed help. As missionaries, they hiked for hours or days into mountain villages to share the gospel. Churches began to develop, and they became overseers. Then the government church heard about it and attempted to destroy the work.

"Do you want to help this couple?" Steven asked.

"YES," I said with enthusiasm and this time no sense of danger. *They were the ones* going into the dangerous areas!

We made a trip to see them and take some audio Bibles for villagers who couldn't read. After hours on the road, we arrived at a point where we needed to abandon the vehicle. Then we walked across a swinging bamboo bridge where we met up with farmers on the other side. They would take us the rest of the way on motorcycles.

We rode on the back of their bikes bouncing and sliding on the dirt road through the mountains. 'Are we there yet?' took on a new meaning as I thought it each time we passed different villages. Finally, we stopped at a river bank.

"Is this their house?" I asked, as we got off the bikes near a large shack.

"No. Their house is over there," they pointed. "We have to go across the river."

The current of this muddy river was rushing by with great force. The sound of the flowing water seemed to dare us to "just try and come across." Recent rains had elevated the waters to such a point that even Steven was nervous about it, and he typically feared nothing.

Minister Zhang waited for us on his narrow bamboo raft. "It will be fine," he said, reassuring us that he could get us across. He was used to hooking his rod to a line that went across the river and directing the raft to the other side. We trusted him and got on. The travel across was about the length of two football fields.

After the exhilarating ride, we arrived at our host's humble house, an open structure set on stilts at the base of a mountain. There were no other houses in sight. Just lush banana trees, rubber trees and various livestock. It wouldn't be the most comfortable night, with no bathroom or even an outhouse, but we agreed to stay and do some teaching in the morning. Our motorcycle friends planned to come and bring other farmers from the area.

Zhang and his wife were two of the most precious Christians one could meet. It was amazing how we could fellowship and connect with each other even though we were cultures apart.

"We are so excited that you're here," they told me. "We are always going everywhere to encourage others, but no one ever comes to encourage us."

Everything was pleasant until after dinner when it began to RAIN. Here we go again! How would the rain affect our ability to leave the next day? Apart from crossing the river, there was no way out.

"Oh, don't worry," the wife said. "It has rained every night for the past two months. It will stop in a short while. It won't make things worse." That was a relief.

However, the relief was short lived. The rain began to come down heavy.

"It hasn't rained this hard in a long time!" they said.

That sick feeling came into my stomach. The rain kept pouring. As we laid down to sleep around midnight, the rain was still consistent. Learning my lesson from Burma, I resisted panic and was able to sleep a little bit. Even so, I still battled with various fears and emotions that night.

The next morning Zhang was up early. He surveyed the outside and began cooking breakfast. When I got up, he greeted me with, "The river is too high. We won't be able to cross it this morning."

"How long will it take to go down?" I asked.

"Maybe later this afternoon. If not, maybe tomorrow morning."

That didn't sound good. What if it rained again?

It was going to be a long day. There would be no meeting with the other farmers, because they couldn't cross the river either.

The day began overcast, but the sun eventually shined. Although the weather got hot, the river didn't go down enough. We would have to stay another night. It wasn't fun to think that we could be stuck there for weeks if it continued to rain in the evenings.

I called Pete and told him the situation. He just laughed. It wasn't the first time I had called with a predicament, and he knew the Lord would get me out just like the other times. But I didn't think it was very funny at the moment!

Then, after that call, it started to drizzle. That was the last thing we needed! Then the drizzle worked up to a moderate shower. That's when I called another friend, Doug Lichtwark in Kunming.

"I could use some prayers, Doug," I said, and told him the situation.

The New Zealander prayed with me over the phone: "Father we pray that you redirect the rain so that the river gets no higher, that there would be no more rain where Rick is tonight, and that he would be able to get out of there tomorrow, in Jesus' name!"

We chatted a little after that, and by the time we finished the call, the rain had stopped falling.

That was a good start, but the whole night was ahead. As I laid down to sleep, my ears tuned into every sound, wondering if it was a drop of rain. The sound of the running river was constant, so I listened closely for anything that might be happening on our roof. There wasn't much sleep that night.

Finally at dawn, I rejoiced in the Lord that it hadn't rained the entire evening! Yet Zhang came back with the news that "the river is still not safe to cross."

My heart sank. The thought of staying another day was challenging enough, but it could be several days before the river lowered. There were people to see back in Kunming, and a return flight to catch before too long.

I went outside to pray, hoping to get over the feeling of being trapped. Outside, the choice had to be made: give in to feelings of helplessness, or encourage oneself in the Lord. I had learned to resist the former and practice the latter. All I could think to do was to sing that old song, *"God will make a way, when there seems to be no way..."* It wasn't sung joyfully or well, but it was the best I could do. Then I went back in inside.

Zhang's wife said, "Come to the table, let's eat!"

"Go on and eat without me," I said. "I don't have much of an appetite."

She said, "But you can go home today!"

I did a double take. "What? How?"

Zhang smiled and said, "If we hike two kilometers up to the next village, they have a raft line there, and the water may be safer. We can go and look after lunch."

The clouds gathered as we hiked. When we got to the village no one was there, and we had to wait for someone to show up. While we waited, Zhang inspected the water and the raft. The river was too high, but it was much calmer at this spot, so he decided to proceed.

As he positioned the raft with the line, he encountered a problem. I couldn't understand what the trouble was, but an adjustment had to be made. It caused him notable difficulty, and the delay caused suspense as the clouds kept moving in.

Eventually, he fixed it and got us floating across.

It was a miracle that the rain had stopped the night before. Had the river been any higher, even crossing at that point wouldn't have been safe enough. But God made a way when there seemed to be no way.

On the other side of the river, the motorcycles carried us back to town. I had never been happier bouncing and sliding on dirt roads.

Chapter 22

Preaching and Teaching Tours

"We want you to come and teach our people."

We heard this from several Chinese pastors as Pete and I traveled through northern parts of China. Most of these pastors had suffered greatly for the gospel. In earlier days they were thrown in jail, kicked and beaten because they would not renounce their faith. It was very humbling that THEY should be asking US to teach them, when they had suffered so much and yet proved faithful. These were the superstars.

In heaven the true celebrities will be revealed. They won't necessarily be the ones who preached awesome sermons or sold thousands of books. They will be the ones who held onto God when all else was against them. They will be the unknowns who remained faithful when it would have been easier to give up or go after the world.

Nonetheless, it was good that we should teach them. The Lord had blessed us with a revelation of grace that we knew would bless them, and which they needed to hear. They didn't have access to all the resources we have in the west. There are so many teaching materials available in America, including books, television, and other media, that it would be impossible to exhaust it all. Not so in China. Most Chinese Christians do not have access to resources that can encourage their faith. So we considered ourselves to be living resources.

We taught at meetings set up by Chinese church leaders. Bible-hungry believers came from villages as far as 100 kilometers away to hear the Word of God. In one place it got so packed, it felt like the book of Acts. People sat in the window sills and crowded outside to hear us.

In some areas we had to travel by night to avoid being noticed. In one place we were basically confined to our small rooms for three days, only coming out at times to teach and to eat.

We did some crazy traveling, but one trip took the prize. I had to record the details in my journal:

Travel details. May 2011. We flew for 3 hours and then drove for 3 hours to the first place. Spent four nights there. Then took a 4 hour train to the next place and stayed four nights. Then took a 1 hour train and got in a car for another hour to get to the next place. Stayed two nights. Next we rode a bus for 6 hours and spent two nights in that place.

Then we took a car for 4 hours to the next place, and in two spots we had to detour along the way because of modern day road bandits who were blocking the road with heavy machinery. They demanded money if we wanted to get straight through. So we backed up and added another hour to the drive. We stayed three nights and then took a bus 4 1/2 hours to the last place, and two days later flew back home on a 2 1/2 hour flight.

I'm just thankful for modern travel. In times past, missionaries traveled for days on oxcarts and donkeys and stayed in worse places. And lives were often lost to the road bandits.

Pete and I often felt the presence of heaven in the little dumps we stayed in. God brought revival to many weary souls. Many confessed that their lives were changed, and several people were healed.

One day an older lady came to me after a session and asked for prayer.

"My back hurts and my legs hurt!" She motioned to the different places on her body.

I prayed for her, and she walked away. Later that day she came back and we went through it all over again.

"My back hurts and my legs hurt!"

She insisted that I pray again, so I did.

The next day, she went to Pete and asked for prayer for the same thing. He prayed and she walked away. And like the day before, she came back later and said, "Pray for me!"

At that time, we had just finished praying for a young man who was mentally handicapped. This fellow had been disrupting the meetings. He would get up and move around and make noises. His father would chase him around to get him to quiet down. During a break in the sessions, Pete rebuked a demonic spirit that was influencing the boy, and then we prayed for him.

Pete ministered to the boy, and spoke life over him. As he encouraged the boy to smile and worship the Lord, the lady came again demanding prayer.

I reminded her, "We've prayed for you already, several times." But with the small group present, we all laid hands on her, and Pete took the boy's hand and put it on her as well. After prayer, she walked away and the young man felt like he had just done something very important. And he no longer disrupted the meetings.

At the end of the day, I saw the lady and asked how she was.

"All better!" she said.

The next day I asked her again just to make sure we were both talking about her body. "How's the pain?"

"All better! Praise the Lord!"

It wasn't just the preaching and praying that had effect on so many. It was the love of God. "The greatest of these is love" (1Cor.13:13). Everywhere we went, I saw the power of love making a difference. Sometimes just a hug or a few words of encouragement would visibly affect the Chinese.

The culture was changing. In the past, it wouldn't be proper to show outward expressions of love, like giving hugs. But the church ate it up and started to show it in return. Those meetings changed me as much as anybody else. Faith rises up in an atmosphere of love. "Faith works by love" (Galatians 5:6).

We met believers who had so little, yet their faces shined like angels. One leader, Mr. Jia, stood out among others. He stood out because he laid low. He was a quiet man and didn't try to put on any airs. He had spent a year in jail for his faith. We asked him, "Did you sense any special help from the Holy Spirit during that time?"

He smiled and replied, "I couldn't have survived otherwise."

He stayed after our meetings and actually helped to sweep and clean up. Most leaders left that for others in the church. But Mr. Jia was always ready to serve.

If we needed anything, he was on it before we had a chance to ask. I would be putting on my coat, and he was right there to help get it on. I would reach over the table for some salt, and he would grab hold of my sleeve so it didn't drop in the soup. He seemed more attentive to us than we were to ourselves. All the while, Pete and I admired him as a quiet and humble man.

But on the night that we left, he gave each of us a hug as we got into the van. When we pulled away, Pete and I looked at each other, and one of us said, "Who was that guy?"

It dawned on us as we drove away that this was a GREAT man of God. Tears welled up as we realized it. It was as if we had just been in the presence of Jesus Himself.

We were connected with one of the largest underground church movements in China. There are reportedly five major networks. These networks are amazing as far as how widespread and connected they can get throughout the country. This group had workers all over China, and we could be busy until the end if we were able to travel to all their locations.

That said, most of this modern church movement is still very much in an infant stage. Many of the leaders are only a few pages ahead of their people. In some places, the wives of young leaders, still kids themselves, teach countryside students in their hidden Bible schools.

The students come and live together in crowded quarters for two years. They eat mostly rice, eggs, and vegetables because it is too costly to provide meat every day. Maybe once a week they get to eat some pork.

It was a privilege to be able to visit and encourage different Bible school students. Some of them were as young as 12 and others over 40. Most of them had never interacted with a foreigner before. We were cultures apart, and yet the love of Christ bonded us.

Preaching and teaching took off on the home front as well. Back in Kunming, I worked with several house church Bible schools. One school was different in that it was made up of educated city people. That was a fun one. We had all kinds of lively discussions, as I shared the reviving truths of the gospel with them. They had a more traditional and academic approach to the Bible. They were used to dry and dusty theological lectures, mostly from other Asian missionaries. They didn't know what to make of me at first. The way westerners teach is different than the way Asians teach, in any subject. On top of that, I came in and challenged a lot of their traditions.

But after a few weeks, they began to eat it all up. They came alive. Again, it was simply that I was passing along *what had made me come alive.* The goal was that they would in turn take it to others: "And the things that you have heard from me among many witnesses, commit these to faithful men who will be able to teach others also" (2Timothy 2:2). They eventually did.

I created a discipleship curriculum to teach outside of the Bible schools. The goal was to get small group leaders materials to duplicate and teach to others. I met with one group weekly at the wrong time and in the wrong place.

It was the wrong time because it was right after lunch when everyone was sleepy.

It was the wrong place because we met in a dark room with no windows.

It was frustrating because people came inconsistently. It was hard to build upon each lesson when different ones missed, and new ones showed up. I tried to make it as lively as possible, and my translator, Miss Zhao, was in step every bit of the way. We practically sang and danced, but the group's response was, for the most part, sleepy.

Well, that was a failure, I thought. After several weeks, it didn't seem to accomplish anything. But to my surprise, I later learned that my translator, Miss Zhao, had been teaching the material to her own church group.

"My group loves this material, and I'm having so much fun teaching it to them!" she exclaimed.

Once again, God was working when appearances suggested otherwise.

Chapter 23

Old Missionary, New Hope

The heat was on. China had been slowly cooking up pressure for the church. A British friend was forced to leave after years of work on a college campus. I was invited to work with a new Chinese brother, and the police began to threaten him.

The country seemed to be moving backwards. The government blocked access to outside information, including any website not submitted to Chinese control. No more Facebook or You Tube. Sometimes it was difficult to even receive email. We had to install a VPN (Virtual Private Network) in order to get around the great firewall of China.

The Lord was still moving, and opportunities to travel and teach continued, but the down times in between were too long. I struggled with how to fill the time. It was getting costly to travel so much, and our financial support wasn't keeping up with the rising expenses.

Meanwhile, Jennifer started traveling back to the States to help care for her aging grandmother, a precious lady who outlived all of her children.

The question confronted us: is it time to move on? We had considered the possibility for several years, but we always put it off. Now, after 18 years of serving in China, it seemed we had to make the choice.

Maybe I could have done better, but I had done everything I knew to try to keep us there. Doors continued to shut. Finances kept drying up. It was like the Lord was saying, "Go," even though we didn't hear Him saying, "Come." We didn't know where we would end up. It just seemed it was time to go.

Although it wasn't clear what would happen when we left, we felt like the lepers in Samaria who sat at the gate after the Syrians attacked. "They said to one another, 'why are we sitting here until we die?'" (2Kings 7:3). They might be killed by the Syrians if they left, but it was certain they'd die if they stayed. So they took a chance. They got up and went to the Syrian camp, only to find that no one was there. The Lord had caused the Syrians to flee, and the lepers found all the valuables!

The decision was made. It's time to go.

Thus began a great crisis. For months, I saw the day approaching but had no clear direction past landing in America. What would we do? Where would we live? How would I support a family of five? As the day got closer, the burden got heavier. I wasn't hearing from the Lord.

Yet at the same time He seemed to be confirming the move. Two Chinese brothers encouraged me and affirmed that God would use us in another context. I thought Steven would take it hard that I was leaving. However, he surprised me with his response: "We will miss you, but you don't need to be here long term anymore.

"The things you and others have helped us to do, we can do them now. The Chinese church has grown. You can come back and teach for a few weeks at a time, but there is no reason to keep your family here now." In this sense it seemed like we had worked ourselves out of a job, which is really what missionaries should aspire to do.

We also met with others for prayer each week, and one night a couple prophesied over us. "You don't know your next assignment but God is getting it ready. There are people waiting for you and praying for you to come. You will be an answer to their prayers and bless them, and they will be a blessing to you."

That was encouraging. But I still had no idea what I was supposed to do next.

The temptation to give in to fear was great. At times it was almost overwhelming. These passages kept me from falling, and became my continual battle cries in prayer:

> **Proverbs 3:6:** Acknowledge Him in all your ways and He will direct your paths.

> **Jeremiah 29:11:** But I know the thoughts that I think toward you, says the LORD, thoughts of peace and not of evil, to give you a future and a hope.

> **Psalm 31:19:** Oh how great is Your goodness, which you have laid up for those who fear You, which you have prepared for those who trust in You in the presence of the sons of men!

> **Isaiah 46:4:** Even to your old age I am He; and even to gray hairs will I carry you: I have made, and I will bear; even I will carry, and will deliver you.

It got really intense when we bought our plane tickets to go home, and still didn't know where we were going to end up. I needed to hear from God.

And then one night, with about a month left to go, I recalled what a friend told me of a time when he needed direction. He said, "I sat down and told the Lord, 'God I need to hear from you. If I have to sit three minutes *or three weeks,* I'm not moving from this chair until I hear Your voice!'"

I asked the Lord, "Is that what I have to do? Am I going to have to sit and not move until I hear your voice?"

Quiet.

Then a sense of warmth came upon my heart, and I just knew He wasn't asking me to do that. "No," I said, "You love me. I know it will all be okay..."

WHAM! The Spirit of God overwhelmed me and started imparting vision.

Up until then, I thought I was finished. Now I sensed, "You're not finished. You're just beginning. The things you've been doing here you can continue to do. You just don't need to live here now, you can come and go. Besides that, you can go to other countries as well. But you will be based in the States, where they need to hear this message too."

Finally! I had some direction. "But Lord," I asked, "what about in the States? What will I do there, and where?"

He seemed to be saying *a church or ministry.*

A church? What church? Or did He mean some other ministry group? Did He mean pastor, or associate pastor? But I heard nothing more. It was enough, however, to settle me. The crisis was over.

A few days later, I received a text from Pete, who happened to be in Missouri. "Rick, there's a small storefront church here looking for a pastor. They asked me if I could do it, but I told them about YOU."

Well that didn't take long! But the prospect dimmed when he told me the name of the church.

"New Hope Lutheran Church."

I texted back, "ARE YOU CRAZY?" Nothing against Lutherans. Just not our style.

"Relax," he wrote, "they're Lutheran in name only." *That wasn't true.* "And they are really hungry for the Word." *That WAS true.*

It was a group of retirees who had left the main Lutheran church in the area because of its acceptance of homosexuality in the pulpit. The New Hope group didn't hate homosexuals, but they knew that the Bible condemned the practice.

I thought it wouldn't hurt to send them an email. They were okay with the fact that I wasn't a Lutheran. They perused my website, saw what I taught, and still invited me to come and preach. So we planned to visit early on when we got to the States.

We arrived at Lake of the Ozarks, Missouri. It was so different from China, of course, but also from any place I was used to in the States. We were still fighting jetlag and wondering what we were doing in this foreign country.

Bill and Nancy Moore met us and prepared me for a meeting with the church board the next day. Bill spoke of the Lutheran council and other "governmental" talk about how we could possibly make this work. I just thought, "How did I get into this?"

The meeting with the board was awkward at first. So there wouldn't be any misunderstandings, I made it clear and upfront that I could never be a Lutheran. I had to know that they were okay with that.

The discussion continued with talk of a temporary arrangement that would be mutually beneficial. They would allow me to continue making trips to China, and I would be their pastor during the times at home.

Then at some point in the meeting, everyone loosened up and seemed like family. The Holy Spirit entered in, and we all started to laugh and enjoy each other's company. At the end, everyone seemed okay with me, the "non-denominational."

Then I preached on Sunday. Before I spoke, they ran through a full blown Lutheran liturgy. Jennifer and I sat there thinking *we could never do this.* Yet they were hungry for the Word.

Afterward at lunch, they more or less pleaded us to come back and pastor the church. But as we drove away, we both agreed—a Lutheran liturgy week after week just wasn't for us.

We didn't want to hurt their feelings, so we tried to get *them* to shut the door. I texted Bill, "Maybe there's a better choice for you out there," and listed some discrepancies we had with Lutheranism.

When I sent the text, my heart sank. For some reason, it made me sad.

There was no reply for hours. But when the reply came, it said, "Please don't give up on us."

It started to look like the Lord was in on this.

New Hope Church turned out to be the group that was prophesied to us. They were the ones who had been praying for us to come, and they became such a blessing in our lives.

But it almost didn't happen. The board had to deal with a member who wanted strictly Lutheran. It seemed they couldn't get through to him and were ready to give up. At a Bible study, Bill and some others decided it would be best to call everything off. But just before they finished meeting, Lois Gonseth received a call.

"Oh Hi, Larry," she answered. "No, I didn't call you."

Larry had been advising the church from a distance. Lois put him on the speaker phone.

"I know that one of your parishioners is objecting," he said with great conviction, "but listen, don't you let that missionary go. GOD HAS SENT HIM to you, and that all the way from China!"

After the call, Lois looked as if she'd seen a ghost. She hadn't called Larry, and she didn't even have his number in her phone! None of them had talked to him about the objecting member either. They all took it as a directive from the Lord.

That settled it. They took a bold step of faith and called me to be their "Non-denominational Missionary Shepherd."

After time, the member who tried to get rid of us became one of our biggest friends. And when he and his wife moved away to another State, they ended up joining a non-denominational church.

Chapter 24

Abundant God

The church and I agreed that my role as Non-denominational Missionary Shepherd would last for a two-year term. They were blessed to have a pastor. We were blessed that they gave us a part-time salary and allowed me to make periodic trips to China.

The Lutherans had told me they were willing to make some changes to their services.

"Be gentle" was the counsel I received from others. "Don't try to change them too quickly."

It seemed like good advice. However, as soon as we got there, the worship committee asked for my input. I didn't want to push anything. I simply told them what I thought. Changes took place immediately, and our first service was significantly less liturgical.

Over time, more changes took place. Some folks were understandably unhappy. But many were coming alive to the things of God like never before.

After a few months, Bill's wife Nancy came bursting with something to tell me. "I don't have to be a Lutheran anymore! Isn't that funny? Me, of all people!" She had been one all her life. Nancy and others were discovering God in a way that transcended tradition and religion.

It's not wrong to be a Lutheran or a part of any other Christian denomination. What's wrong is when the denomination itself is more important than a growing relationship with God. Many miss the power of God because they see no further than the religious ways they have grown accustomed to, "making the word of God of no effect through your tradition which you have handed down" (Mark 7:13). Jesus upset the religious order of His day, and brought life in the process. The Word will do the same today to those who let it.

That first year I went to China twice, and also to Honduras and Bulgaria. Each time in China was like picking up without missing a beat. Over the next three years I would see the Lord doing as great and even greater works through these trips than when we lived there.

Yet there was constant financial tension. We hadn't really lost much support when we moved back to America, which was typically unheard of. In fact, we even gained some support. But the cost of living here was higher than in China, and the travels drained our finances quickly. Yet God was faithful. Sometimes the money didn't come in when we thought we needed it, but it always eventually came. In Mississippi, Pastor Bob Pugh encouraged me with stories of his own past financial challenges, and how God came through with ABUNDANCE.

Then one day in prayer, God gave me a tremendous revelation of His abundant nature. I had been recording podcasts for the internet, and He gave me a great teaching. The gist of it was that everything God does is extravagant. He doesn't just love us, He loves us over the top! When He told the disciples to put their nets out for a catch, their net overloaded and broke. When He fed the five thousand by multiplying the fish and the loaves, there were twelve basketfuls of leftovers. Some might consider that a waste. The point is that He goes overboard with abundance.

He didn't just create a few stars, or few grains of sand, and His thoughts to us are more numerous than the sand (Psalm 139:18). He didn't just save us, but gave us His own Son, that we might have not just part, but an entire kingdom!

So why do we worry about making ends meet? Our loving Father is abundant towards us. Yet in this revelation, I was taught to look to HIM as my abundance, not necessarily what was in my hand. Abundance is His nature. And He loves me with such abundant love that it surpasses knowledge (Ephesians 3:19). Worry and fear develop because we tend to look at *what we need* more than WHO HE IS, our abundantly loving Father.

Why fall out of whack when for the moment there seems to be a problem? The over the top love of God cannot help but see us through. Faith will grab on to this when sight suggests otherwise.

Greatly encouraged, I prepared for the next China trip. When Jennifer and I visited our sending organization's home office, I asked the finance person for an update on our funds.

"How much do we have in our account, Marla? I need to pull some out for China."

"Let me see..." she clicked through some files. "Here it is." And she gave me the total.

I stared blankly. It wasn't that much.

I made calculations in my head. *It might work. I could squeak by with it.* But I couldn't be generous with it. In China we like to help our brothers and sisters and bless them financially. We like to pay for them when they travel with us. And it's better to bring too much than too little. This was enough to just get by minimally. Apart from that, there would be no money left to pay our upcoming rent and a huge tax bill that was due soon.

I had her write the check. Then I walked into an empty room and looked up to heaven.

"That's not good enough!" I said reverently, but boldly. "That's not who you are! That's not what you taught me about your abundant nature!" I gave thanks anyway and ended with praise. Then I visited others in the office and smiled to hide my disappointment.

The next day the hissy fit was over. I told the Lord I still believed everything. Even if I had nothing else, I had everything in Him. We would be okay. I didn't know where the rent or tax money was going to come from, but assumed we'd have it at some point.

When the plane took off for China, fear and worry started to hit.

"NO!" I answered back to the devil. "I'm not going to even think about this. God will provide." There were a few weeks left for money to come in. It's just that our track record hadn't been so good lately.

One of the deans of a Chinese Bible school offered to pick me up at the airport. I told her she shouldn't do that because getting to the airport is a chore, and it would be late at night. But she insisted, saying a former student wanted to see me.

It was almost midnight when my 20 plus hours of travel concluded in Kunming. The dean was there to meet me with a young man.

"This is your student's son," she said. "Your student couldn't make it tonight. She had business out of town."

Walking through the airport, we made small talk. The dean asked if I could read Chinese. I told her yes and demonstrated. I pointed to a sign and read it wrong.

"I'm just sleepy, forgive me!" Then I read another one correctly.

"Oh very good," she said. "How about handwritten? Can you read handwritten Chinese?"

"If it's simple and neat," I answered.

The boy dropped her off and took me to the hotel. When we arrived, he pulled my suitcase out of the trunk and said goodbye. But before I got away, he stopped me.

"Wait! I almost forgot. My mother wanted to give you a gift." He pulled out a bag, and I took it and thanked him. I figured it might be some tea or a friendship plaque of some sort. At least that's what the gifts usually are.

Even though it was past midnight, there was a line at the reservation desk for the hotel. After waiting a few minutes, I remembered the gift. *Wonder what it is,* I thought, and looked inside the bag.

It wasn't tea.

Was I seeing correctly?

Inside were four thick stacks of money.

That woke me up! I quickly closed the bag and looked around to see if anyone was watching. Then the questions started flying in my head. *What does she want with me? Is this supposed to go to someone else? Was this a mistake?*

In my room I looked in the bag again. I found a note in handwritten Chinese, two pages long, but could only understand about 40% of it. It looked like it might be an offering for me, but I just couldn't accept anything until I knew for sure. It was an extraordinary amount of money. From the looks of it, it would more than cover my time in China as well as pay our upcoming rent and tax bill. I wept at the thought of it.

The next day I called the dean. Now I knew why she asked if I could read Chinese. Because my Chinese is limited, I didn't understand everything she said, but it seemed the student had a successful year in business and wanted to bless me. The dean assured me it was a gift, and that I should receive it.

Later my translator helped me with the letter. The first page spoke of how this woman had been blessed learning about God in our Bible classes. The next page spoke of how she had felt led to give us a gift before we moved back to the States. At that time, she didn't follow through. More recently, she had thought about it, felt bad, and prayed that God would give her another chance. Then she heard that I was coming back on this trip.

"This is God's money," she wrote, "you don't have to thank me."

The miracle in this was two-fold. It was to date the largest offering I had received. I was able to cover the trip AND take care of things at home. But it was also amazing that it came from a Chinese student. The Chinese church was still very young in understanding the concept of supporting missionaries. They rarely gave offerings, let alone huge ones. That said, the dean told me this faithful woman had been tithing even before her business took off.

God has always been faithful and ABUNDANT. That doesn't mean that we didn't have hard months after that. We did. And trials are always abundant. But there's always hope. God, The Grace Agent, continues to work, though sometimes we don't perceive it.

It's helpful to remember that it's not only by faith, but also in PATIENCE that we receive the promises (Heb. 6:12). If we trust in who God is, more than in what we have, we will eventually have all we need, in order to reflect who He truly is.

After an abundant two years with the church in Missouri, it was time to move on. We moved to Mississippi for a season to help with Jennifer's aging grandmother.

The ministry continues, with travels back and forth to China and various preaching and teaching in the States. The future is open, and we wait to see what is revealed in the next chapter that God has for our lives.

He is not anti-climactic. The adventure continues for us all, and the best is yet to come...

Stay Connected!

View

More photos from China

Read

Faith-building articles

Listen

To inspiring podcasts

Subscribe

To our newsletter

Support

The ministry

ricksbell.com

Other Books By Rick...

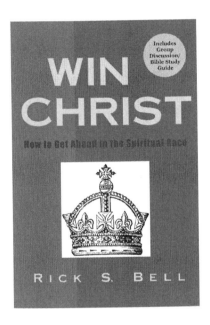

Having faith means more than holding traditions, morals and values. *Win Christ* presents a model for grace, victory and power in the spiritual life. The Biblical truths, combined with personal experiences and historic anecdotes, will inspire and encourage readers both young and old.

Includes a Group Discussion and Bible Study guide.

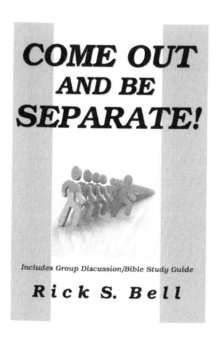

COME OUT AND BE SEPARATE!

Includes Group Discussion/Bible Study Guide

Rick S. Bell

Believers need to stand out and shine in these dark times, and they can! It doesn't happen by religious determination, but by knowing the truth and being set free.

This message is written for all who would desire this. Both challenging and encouraging, it provides practical considerations for moving forward in the Christian faith.

Includes a Group Discussion and Bible Study guide.

THE ONE WHO OVERCOMES

PERSEVERANCE AND VICTORY
IN THE BOOK OF REVELATION

RICK S. BELL

Passing by the speculations and concentrating on the spiritual truths behind the prophecy, *The One Who Overcomes* presents the book of Revelation in an easy to understand and practical manner.

This is *not* an analysis of how current events line up with Biblical prophecy. Instead, it is a look at Revelation in terms of what the believer can use *now* in his or her spiritual journey.

62942448R00105

Made in the USA
Lexington, KY
22 April 2017